FUN WITH FLOWERS

To Joyce
Always... Flowers!

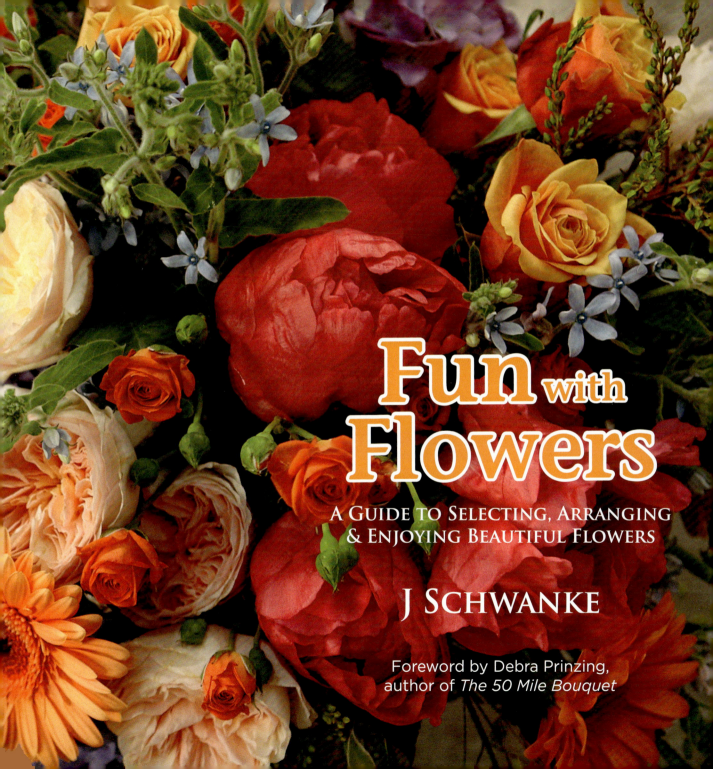

Fun with Flowers

A Guide to Selecting, Arranging & Enjoying Beautiful Flowers

J Schwanke

Foreword by Debra Prinzing,
author of *The 50 Mile Bouquet*

Fun with Flowers
A Guide to Selecting, Arranging & Enjoying Beautiful Flowers

Copyright © 2014 by J Schwanke

Flower Arrangements and Text by J Schwanke

Photography by Dean Van Dis Photo
Dean Van Dis, Joe Matteson and Andrew Maguire

All rights reserved. No part of this book may be reproduced, stored, or transmitted in any form without permission in writing from the publisher, except by a reviewer who may quote brief passages for review purposes.

ISBN-978-0-615-92690-2

Library of Congress Control Number: 2013922160
CIP information available upon request

First Edition, 2014

J Schwanke Productions • Comstock Park MI 49321
616.446.6086 • www.uBloom.com • j@uBloom.com

Book Design - Kelly James Blank, Blank Art and Design
Editor - Pamela McCormick, Digital Ink Services

Additional Photos
pages 24, 34, 35, 84 and 85 by Kelly Blank
pages 5, 13, 18, 31, 32 and 36 courtesy of the Schwanke Family

Printed by Custom Printers and bound by Dekker Book,
in Grand Rapids, Michigan, USA.

Printed on Endurance Gloss post-consumer recycled paper by Xpdex,
FSC Chain-of-Custody Certified.

Arrive Alive is a registered trademark of MAC Technologies. Color Fresh is a registered trademark of FernTrust, Inc. David Austin is a registered trademark of David Austin Roses. Deco Beads is a registered trademark of JRM Chemical, Inc. Design Master is a registered trademark of Design Master color tool, Inc. Gala Bouquet Holder is a registered trademark of FloraCraft Corporation. Swiss Army is a registered trademark of Victorinox AG.

Dedication

To Dorothy Swanson...
who taught me to live life to its fullest...
without reservation.
And to always laugh from the tips of my toes.

To Carnation Joe Green...
who taught me the fine art of Storytelling...
and reminded me to never let the truth stand in
the way of a good story.

To Kelly...
You are the "Perfect Flower" for this "Vase"...
Filling my life daily with Charm, Insight, Humor and Wisdom...
Life with You is constantly Better!

CONTENTS

FOREWORD
Every Flower Tells a Story — 9

INTRODUCTION
Fun with Flowers... and J! — 10

FUN WITH FLOWERS PROJECTS

Fun with Tulip Tree Flowers — 16
Fun with the Flower Food Groups — 20
Fun with Stock Flowers — 22
Fun with a Carnation Pavé Tray — 26
Fun with Daisy Pompons — 28
Fun with Red Carnations — 30
Fun with Terrariums — 34
Fun with Submerged Flowers — 38
Fun with Pin Cushion Protea — 40
Fun with Calla Lillies — 44
Fun with Rose Lillies — 46
Fun with Emoticon Mums — 50
Fun with Composite Flowers — 52
Fun with Single Flowers — 56
Fun with Wedding Flowers — 60
Fun with Orchid Garlands — 62
Fun with Flowers for Pets — 64
Fun with Mercury Glass — 68
Fun with Orchid Stems — 72
Fun with Iris and Ginger — 74
Fun with Tulips on the Bulb — 76
Fun with Fruit and Flowers — 80
Fun with Vegetables and Flowers — 82
Fun with Sunflowers — 86
Fun with Ombré Colors — 90
Fun with Changing Colors — 92
Fun with Complementary Colors — 96
Fun with Rainbow Colors and Flowers — 98
Fun with Black Roses — 100
Fun with Roses — 104
Fun with Aspidistra Leaves — 108
Fun with Weaving Palm Leaves — 110
Fun with Protea and Texture — 112
Fun with Waterproof Ribbon — 114
Fun with Succulents — 116
Fun with Orchid Plants — 122
Fun with Pumpkins — 124
Fun with Recycling Wine Bottles — 126
Fun with Christmas Flowers — 128
Fun with Fragrant Flowers — 130
Fun with Art and Flowers — 134

FAVORITE FLOWERS

Stock — 25
Rose Lily — 49
Clematis — 67
Tree Peony — 95
Succulents — 119
Stemmed Gardenia — 133

FLOWER FRIENDS

"Carnation Joe" Green & his Lily — 32
Ismael Resendiz — 42
Kim Carson — 58
Lane DeVries — 78
Jenna Arcidiancono — 84
Lily Garcia — 106

FLOWERS 101

Where Do Flowers Come From? — 18
Growing Flowers to Arrange — 36
Finding Flowers to Arrange — 54
The Secrets to Longer Lasting Flowers — 70
The Right Flower Arranging Tools — 88
Ideas on Working with Color — 102
Flower Arranging Vessels — 120

Resource Guide — 136

Acknowledgements — 142

Contributors — 143

About uBloom.com — 144

Fun with Flowers   7

FOREWORD | Debra Prinzing

Every Flower Tells a Story.

That is, if you carefully observe and listen to the amazing narrative it has to share. There's much to learn from flowers, especially if you're inquisitive, looking past the inherent beauty of a stem, leaf, petal or pod to study the history of a plant species.

Take that curiosity further and ask "where did it originate?" or "who are the people who brought this flower to life?" And finally, inspired by that flower's splendor and origins, you take that stem in your hands… combine it with other stems that have equally amazing stories to tell… and create a botanical arrangement deserving of admiration and wonder.

How many designers do you know who care enough about the universe of flowers to ask all those questions before ever filling a vase with water or cutting a single stem? The name J Schwanke is synonymous with flowers and floral design. In today's instant-gratification world, where many people only see flowers at the grab-and-go bucket next to the check-out line, he is reconnecting consumers and industry insiders alike to the amazing character and influence of flowers in our lives.

Open the pages of this book or watch him in action and you'll soon realize that J enthusiastically promotes not just flowers but the people who grow and design with them. I'm so impressed with his passion, his telegenetic personality and his ability to draw out the stories of flower farmers and others in the floral world.

We have J to thank for changing our relationship with flowers. I really do think flowers are in this man's DNA, from a child-hood spent in greenhouses and the Schwanke family flower shop, to his own amazing career as a floral educator and spokesman.

He has been championing American Grown flowers for so much longer than I have – and I credit J for pioneering the cause that I've also embraced as my own personal mission. He tirelessly trumpets this message – and I'm honored to join with him in promoting the beloved American-grown flower.

Author and speaker, Debra Prinzing is the leading advocate for a sustainable, seasonal and local approach to flower design and is credited with creating the term "Slow Flowers." In 2014 Debra launched www.slowflowers.com, a free online guide to florists, shops and studios who design with American-grown flowers.

10 Fun with Flowers

INTRODUCTION
Fun with Flowers… and J!

I'm J Schwanke and I LOVE flowers! My most treasured memories involve flowers in some way or another. From the moment I entered this world, I was destined to love the beauty of flowers. You see, my mom, a 3rd generation florist, delivered me in the middle of a Nebraska Flower Convention during a snowstorm! Yes. It's true.

I grew up in a family of professional florists in Fremont, Nebraska, smack dab in the middle of the USA, so my parents started me early along the flower path. Whether it was running through our family greenhouses, or "putting up flowers" when they arrived in big boxes from California or picking *Cattails* with my Grandpa and Grandma, "Carnation Joe Green" and his Lily… for me, life has always been "all about the flowers."

My parents are quite famous when it comes to flowers… you may even say that they have "gone viral." My dad is a past president of the Society of American Florists and in the Floriculture Hall of Fame and my mom is a respected Floral Commentator. The world, however, knows them as the "Famous Matching Couple." They were interviewed on the *Today Show*, amongst many other news outlets, for dressing in matching flower themed outfits during their 63 years plus of marriage. Also, my dad never starts a day without his signature *Red Carnation* on his suit coat lapel.

When I decided on a career in flowers, it was no surprise to anyone. My favorite part about flowers is "arranging them." I learned so much from my flower arranging parents, grandparents, aunt and sister as well as "famous" flower

artists and friends I've had the privilege to meet along the way.

Sharing the flowers I've arranged is why I love what I do. I became an expert at "sharing flowers" on the delivery truck in the family business. You realize quickly it's virtually impossible to "ruin" someone's day with flowers. It's an emotional experience; the way their eyes light up, the smile that floods their face... **flowers are simply... Powerful.**

Sharing is a passion... whether it's on my show *Fun with Flowers and J* on uBloom.com, at my hands on workshops or public presentations. People have a natural fondness for flowers and I enjoy sharing the magical things flowers can offer. Flowers are Fun and arranging flowers is easy... you just have to jump in and give it a try!

People often ask, "How do you start an arrangement?" Well for me, it's all about inspiration... and that usually starts with pretty flowers! When you pick up your flower knife, fresh flowers and foliage, something magical happens. Your body actually releases endorphins that create a sense of calm and well-being. You find joy mixing colors, textures, and creating your very own personal flower arrangement. This process repeats each and every time you "arrange flowers."

A single blossom, or collection of blooms, a combination of colors... and then nearly always... I head for a piece of paper... and throw down a quick sketch... it helps me register the 'feeling' I'm heading for solidly into my brain. Then I allow

From a "Bud" to a Bloom

I was welcomed into this world literally surrounded by flowers; I was born at a flower convention! I'm a 4th generation Florist; I grew up in the greenhouses of the family flower business, I played in coolers, bulb caves and flower fields my whole life. I also happen to LOVE arranging flowers.

Being born into an iconic flower family does have its advantages. I owe an abundance of gratitude to my parents, grandparents and great grandparents; together they shared a daily dose of their passion for flowers.

My career in flowers began as a young boy promoting our family flower business. Thanks to my resourceful parents, I starred as "the pitchman" for Greens Greenhouses for the local paper and radio station. This early career path paved the way for a lifetime of amazing flowers, while giving me the foundation needed to express emotion through flower arranging and design.

"Turning people's feelings into flowers" just came naturally and I've been having "Fun with Flowers" ever since.

Watch the video at:
uBloom.com/GreensGreenhouses

Photos of a youngster J when he served as pitchman for Greens Greenhouses in local advertisements.

my hands and brain to connect through the flowers... it's definitely NOT a "science"... it's the "FUN" of translating my inspiration, feelings and emotion with the flowers. It's as simple, and intricate, as that.

Join me as we discover the "Fun with Flowers". I hope it will enrich your life as much as it has mine. I was blessed to be "raised" by inspiring storytellers like my Grandpa, my Aunt Rose and my "babysitter and other mom" Dorothy! I share this because you're about to discover that *Fun with Flowers* is an incredible "collection" of favorite flowers and friends, creative tips and ideas, fun flower projects and best of all; stories from my flower-filled world. Each of the projects in this book has a coordinating "how to arrange flowers" video on my website, uBloom.com. You'll find that watching a "how to video" communicates the "how-to" much better than step-by-step photos. I've listed **FREE links to selected projects** throughout the book. You can visit **uBloom.com**, learn more about those projects and get in on the action.

So my friend, gather up a bunch of colorful flowers, pick up your flower knife, jot down a quick sketch, share a favorite story and get ready for something magical. When flowers and friends come together... there's **Fun with Flowers**... just waiting to happen!

Fun with Tulip Tree Blossoms

Tulip Tree Blossoms are simply magical. They feature bright chartreuse blossoms that reflex backwards to reveal a tangerine water-mark on each petal; while an explosion of stamens surrounds the center of the flower.

With a *Tulip Tree* right outside my kitchen window, Spring is one of my favorite times of the year. I cut my garden flowers early in the morning, just as the sun is rising, to ensure the blossoms are crisp, fresh and hydrated. (Never cut flowers from the garden during the heat of the day.)

My garden flowers include: *Tulip Tree* branches, *Lilacs* and *Yellow Peonies* – that's why I choose to live in Michigan. We have 4 complete seasons. The variations in temperature allow for a multitude of spring blossoms that work great for flower arranging. I sometimes include additional flowers and foliage purchased from my local flower seller to match my garden flowers.

The amazing fragrance of this arrangement fills the air with scents of *Lilac*, *Peony* and *Stock* to welcome Spring in grand fashion.

Color is my favorite design element. I select a color palette based on the flowers I'm using and it always helps in the creative arranging process. **Watch the video at: uBloom.com/TulipTree**

FLOWERS

5 Iris
3 Tulip Tree Branches
5 Yellow Peonies
3 Yellow Pincushion Protea
5 Lilac Stems
2 Stems Craspedia (Globe) Yarrow
5 Yellow Stock
5 Yellow Gerbera Daisies
10 Yellow Ranunculus
3 Bupleurum
5 "Suela" Yellow Roses

FOLIAGE

5 Variegated Aspidistra Leaves
5 Scented Geraniums

AND...

Amethyst Glass Footed Bowl
1 Block Floral Foam
Clear Anchor Tape

Lemon | Olive Bright | Basil | Lavender | Violet

 HINT Never crush stems. Flowers have vascular stems (for the most part) and crushing stems creates blockage, increasing bacteria growth. Instead, cut stems at a 45-degree angle to create the best surface for absorbing water.

Where Do Flowers Come From?

Today's flower business is quite different than it was 100+ years ago (our family business began in 1896!). At one time my family owned nearly 7 acres of glass greenhouses, where we grew virtually everything we sold. We carried a diverse crop of flowers, blooming and green plants. *Roses*, *Carnations*, *Violets* and *Sweet Peas* grew in our greenhouses, *Gladiolus*, *Zinnias*, and *Delphiniums* grew in the fields. Back in the greenhouses, *Chrysanthemums* and *Poinsettias* were timed, shaded and lit to ensure on time blooming. We even had varieties of tropical plants and bedding plants.

CHANGING TIMES

In the 70's California and Colorado became leading flower farming states. Back then, for example, over 150 *Carnations* growers operated in the state of Colorado while thousands of acres of *Carnations* grew in California. Then the USA formed alliances with Columbia and Ecuador to subsidize commercial flower production in South America. Today over 80% of the flowers we consume in the USA come from offshore. There are only a few American producers left.

GLOBAL INFLUENCE

Flower brokers or sellers ship from all around the globe. There's the Famous Dutch Flower Auction in Amsterdam, as well as flower production in Australia, Chile, Russia, and China.

Before the 1960's Greens Greenhouses sold what they grew and grew what they sold. J's mother JoEllen Green Schwanke is pictured at far left with her sisters and Sunflowers.

Even the Middle East gets in the act. Because many varieties are seasonal, airline transportation has opened up availability nearly year round.

PROXIMITY TO MARKET

California is, however, still the USA's largest flower producing state. Because of its unique Mediterranean climate, that has distinct micro-climates perfect for the world's largest varieties of cut flowers, California provides year round flower production. Flowers grown in the USA last longer; they are grown sustainably and support the American economy. Many times of the year California grown flowers are the local choice throughout the USA!

Throughout *Fun with Flowers* you'll see a "Grown in the USA" symbol on projects created entirely with American Grown Flowers and Foliage. It's important to know where your flowers come from. It truly makes a difference!

 TIP Look for the Label! Flower and foliage grown in the USA are typically labeled (i.e. CA Grown). Look for Flowers Grown in the USA to ensure you're getting the highest quality flowers.

Fun with Flowers **19**

Fun with the
Flower Food Groups

Did I mention that I'm a "freak" when it comes to flower care? Different types of flowers do better with specialized flower food. My friends at Chrysal USA are scientists dedicated to making ALL flowers last longer. They have taught me so much about flower care.

Different types of flowers benefit from appropriate (and sometimes specific) flower food to promote longer lasting blooms. (See article on page 70-71). For example, *Roses* do best in food designed for their nutritional requirements. Flowers that come from bulbs or corms perform best in "Bulb Food" which has more food (i.e. sugar) and is designed to allow flowers to open larger, be more colorful and fragrant. *Gerbera Daisies* don't benefit from food as much as they do from clean fresh water, so CVBn Tablets from Chrysal are ideal for keeping bacteria away.

I'm crazy about flowers and love having only one or two types of flowers in a vase. The flower arrangements featured on these pages are called a "mono-typical" because they are made with one type of flower. One benefit of a "mono-typical" arrangement can be color impact. Focusing on one flower type (or two strong colors) makes your arrangement stand out. I like my flowers to get all of the attention!

TIP **Bubble up the color!** *Blue Hydrangeas* are intensified by adding *Chartreuse Viburnum*. Any time you pair "acid green" with another color, it makes that color bubble up and POP!

HINT Placing one flower type in a vase allows you to customize the flower food for best results. When mixing flowers, use a universal flower food made for all types of flowers. Visit **www.chrysalusa.com** for more information.

Fun with Stock Flowers

One of my favorite flowers is *Stock*, also known as "*Gilliflower.*" *Stock* is known for its clove-like fragrance and is available in a wide variety of colors. *Stock* grows best in a specific micro-climate that provides a cool marine layer, like the Lompoc Valley in California.

Ocean View Flowers in Lompoc is one of the world's leading *Stock* producers. During my first visit I witnessed the wonder of *Stock* growing in the fields. The seemingly never-ending stripes of color were an amazing visual. While enjoying the glorious view, a breeze blew across the fields and filled the air with its fragrance. I was speechless and moved to tears. (A moment captured on video by my crew.) It was one of the most beautiful things I have ever experienced.

I've always enjoyed arranging with *Stock*, but my perspective was changed that day, giving me a much deeper appreciation for the flower. Now when I pick up a stem of *Stock*, I remember the bands of color, the multitude of flowers growing, and the fragrant breeze.

When arranging *Stock* flowers I group them by colors in various vases, arranging the vases to mimic how the flowers grow in bands of color in the fields. Using similar vases in different sizes helps unify the collection. I filled the vases with water and cut each bunch all at once with my bunch cutter.

HINT Be sure to remove any foliage that falls below the waterline in the vase to help reduce bacteria.

FLOWERS
10 Stems White Stock
10 Stems Yellow Stock
10 Stems Pink Stock
10 Stems Lavender Stock
10 Stems Purple Stock

AND...
5 Assorted White Ceramic Pots (glazed inside to hold water)

On another visit to Ocean View Flowers… my friends allowed me a "turn on the tractor." Sitting atop a John Deere Tractor in the middle of an American flower field certainly gives you a greater appreciation of the flower farming business.

For a gorgeous centerpiece, place a collection of *Stock* vases down the middle of a table or on a countertop. Perhaps a little breeze will carry the fragrance of the flowers to you; together we can reflect on standing in the *Stock* fields in Lompoc, California surrounded by flowers!

Watch the video at: uBloom.com/StockFlowers

IDEA Groupings of vases can be arranged on a single surface, or spread throughout the house in different locations.

   HINT *Stock* comes in a wide variety of colors, and benefits from "flower food" as well as CVBn tablets (which help reduce bacteria production in water). Keep water off the stock blooms and never mist blossoms. Refresh water every few days.

FAVORITE FLOWERS
Stock

"Stock is ultra-romantic with its delicate paper-like blossoms and delicious fragrance. Colorful, fragrant stock blossoms can simply 'Take you away'."
— J Schwanke

Stock comes in a variety of intense and pastel colors: White, Lavender, Purple, three shades of Pink, two shades of Purple (Royal Purple is pictured), Peach, Cream and Gold.

Stock flowers have a rich flowery fragrance with overtones of clove. According to legend; *Stock* flowers grew in Paradise (Garden of Eden).

Fragrant clusters of 1" tissue-like florets form a flower spike 6-7" long on a stem that's 12-18" in length. These variations in size reflect *Stock's* sensitivity to seasonal conditions.

Scientific Name: Matthiola Incana (ma-THEE-o-la in-KAH-na) Also known as *Gilliflower* or *Alelia* in Spanish.

Stock plants produce both male and female stalks of blooms. While the "female" stem produces seeds, the "male" stem is harvested with very prolific double blossoms.

Flower Meaning: Lasting love, lasting beauty, "You'll always be beautiful to me."

Fun with Stock Flowers

Fun with a Carnation Pavé

I love *Carnations*! Yes, I do. *Carnations* come in a wide variety of colors. They last a long time (whether in a vase or arranged in flower foam) and they also smell good. My family has a long history with them; both my grandfather and father have always worn red *Carnations* in their lapel nearly every day (more about that on page 32). I was surrounded by them almost daily. Growing up I ran in between the benches in our greenhouses that grew *Carnations*.

My friend Chris Martindale, owner of Esprit Miami, also loves *Carnations*. She travels the world searching for amazing flowers. She discovered these colorful *Carnations* in Italy. The colors remind me of Italian ices; they're just yummy.

I created this arrangement using a technique called "pavé." It's a jewelry term introduced into flower design. A pavé of diamonds is a row of diamonds placed close together in a jewelry setting. To do this with flowers, arrange the colorful *Carnations* in rows (cut short and stuck into a 1 inch layer of saturated flower foam) and place close together.

This arrangement will LAST for weeks, because the flowers are short and tightly spaced. The blooms are able to share moisture when they're close together.

Flowers or diamonds you ask? I'll choose flowers every time!

IDEA Pavé Any Flower! Try arranging *Chrysanthemums*, *Daisies*, or even Roses in a pavé for an opulent effect.

FLOWERS
7 Pink Carnations
7 Hot Pink Carnations
7 Gold Carnations
7 Orange Carnations
7 Yellow Carnations
7 Green Carnations

AND...
12" Glass Tray
1 Block of Flower Foam
6 Feet of 2" Wide Chartreuse Ribbon

HINT Conceal the foam and flower stems in this arrangement by tying a wide chartreuse ribbon around the tray. (Remember that acid green makes color bubble up.)

Fun with
Daisy Pompons

Chrysanthemums were a staple in our greenhouses during my childhood. It was the last crop we held on to before the greenhouses were finally dismantled. *Chrysanthemums* require "shading" (i.e. pulling black cloths over the benches each afternoon at the same time to insure blooming).

Chrysanthemums were also disbudded. This meant climbing up ladders to reach the top of the stems, to remove all but ONE bud. This sent the "strength" of the flower to ONE Bud, creating GIANT *Mums* used for homecoming football corsages. For *Spray Chrysanthemums*, we would take out the main bud and allow all the other buds to bloom in order to create a stem with lots of small "pompon-like" flowers. (We referred to these as *Daisy Pompons* because their form resembled a daisy with a yellow or contrasting center).

Pompons come in a nearly endless variety of colors and are long-lasting. Therefore, they are great for flower-shaped projects. For this design, I beveled the edge of the pre-made flower foam heart, cutting the *Pompons* short (an inch or less) and placed them close together to fill in the heart shape.

I positioned the finished *Pompon* heart in a glass tray filled with assorted size Deco Beads® (water storing beads are available at most craft stores). The Deco Bead shapes are a colorful accent to the flowers. For a fun illuminating effect, place small battery operated LED lights beneath the heart and beads.

Anyway you use them; I predict you'll end up agreeing with me... I just ♥ *Pompons*!

FLOWERS
5 Stems Purple Daisy Pompons

AND...
Heart Shaped Flower Foam Form
12" Glass Tray
Assorted Deco Beads in Coordinating Colors

HINT Many flower foam shapes are available; hearts, cones, and spheres. Or you can create your own shape. Cut shapes out of dry foam prior to soaking for best results.

Fun with Red Carnations

The *Carnation* is classic and timeless. It is also now enjoying a resurgence among the "millennial generation" because it is colorful, long lasting, durable, fragrant and affordable, with magnificent traits that make a flower truly valuable.

Far Eastern flower arrangers envy the "Western" line style arrangement shown here. I was fortunate to learn this while studying Ikebana classes in Tokyo in the late 1970's. This project is a typical American style, asymmetrical line arrangement. Students typically learn this style first in flower arranging school.

I arranged these American Grown *Carnations* with accents of foliage (all grown in Central Florida) into saturated flower foam. The line of the arrangement is established by the *Red Carnations*.

This arrangement represents the importance of family or business "roots." The *Red Carnation* is symbolic of my ancestors, heritage and the flower industry, which is so near and dear to my heart.

The *Red Carnations* pictured on these pages are an "Endangered Species." These *Carnations* are some of the LAST American *Carnations*. They were grown by Akiyama Growers (a father and son team) in Watsonville, California. I wore one of these "endangered species" at my wedding in October 2013!

HINT Fluff up the Flower! Often, *Carnations* are shipped before they have opened; you can gently open the blossom of a *Carnation* by pushing back the petals. (Similar to how you fluff a crepé paper flower... remember those?)

FLOWERS
15 Red Carnations

FOLIAGE
2 Stems Curly Willow
3 Stems Leatherleaf
3 "Milky Way" Leaves
2 Aspidistra Leaves
2 Ruscus
2 Variegated Pittosporum
3 Lily Grass
1 Podocarpus

AND...
Green Ceramic Cube Vase
Half a Block of Flower Foam

Flower Legend

Carnation Joe Green & His Lily

Flower Ambassador
Greens Greenhouses, Fremont NE

My grandparents, Carnation Joe and his Lily were famous, especially in the flower world. They loved one another, and they loved a good time. They were "socialites" long before I knew what that term meant. Carnation Joe, in particular, loved a good joke or a story and he had one for nearly every occasion. My Grandpa claimed he was a florist 24 hours a day. He wore a *Red Carnation* every day and "slept with his Lily" at night; a true story that certainly deserved attention.

I was blessed to have my grandparents very involved in my life. We worked together in the flower shop. They took me to school and picked me up every day. I was born on my Grandma's Birthday, March 7, which created a very special bond. Grandma Lil loved a sunset and took to wearing "Sunset" colors for most of her adult life. I watched many a sunset from the back seat of my grandparents' Buick Riveria. They taught me to literally "take time to smell the *Roses*."

Flower legends are rare and Carnation Joe and his Lily were truly legendary!

A love affair with *Red Carnations* is a long family tradition. My grandpa "Carnation Joe" Green was aptly named because he wore a *Red Carnation* every day of his adult life. My dad continues that tradition to this day.

During his tenure as President of the Society of American Florists my father testified to Congress to encourage limited funding of offshore *Carnation* growers. He was unsuccessful. Today nearly 100% all of the *Carnations* sold in the USA are imports!

In 1971, the Governor of Colorado sent a giant football (made exclusively of Colorado Grown *Carnations*) to the Governor of Nebraska to commemorate an outstanding season of Go Big Red Football. ("Go Big Red" is a catchphrase of the University of Nebraska football program.) My dad and grandfather constructed the "football" out of hundreds of American Grown *Carnations*. It was definitely a sight to behold.

We grew *Carnations* in our greenhouses. We also supported many *Carnation* growers in Colorado by purchasing "standing orders" of 1,000 or so every week. We stopped growing them in the 1960's. Throughout the 70's and 80's Colorado and California *Carnation* growers closed their doors, unable to compete with the flood of subsidized (low cost) off shore *Carnations*. Sadly, no *Carnation* growers are left in Colorado.

J and his father, Mel Schwanke pose with a football made of Carnations, which Mel later delivered personally to Nebraska Governor, J.J. Exon.

TIP *Carnations* are sensitive to ethylene. This odorless colorless gas ripens fruit... however ethylene is deadly to *Carnations*! Keep your *Carnations* (and other flowers) away from ripe fruit (especially in closed spaces).

Fun with Red Carnations

Fun with Terrariums

Terrariums are covered glass containers that contain miniature tropical plants. Anything with a lid — bottles, jars, bubble bowls, even apothecary jars; — can become a *Terrarium*. When planted they create a mini-biosphere capable of supporting plant life.

My sister Cindy is the *Terrarium* Queen. As a kid I would imagine living inside the tiny landscapes my sister created; climbing the tiny clay pot stairs, or looking out from the cork vistas. My sister taught me how to create and – more importantly – to love a good *Terrarium*.

Cindy is an avid gardener as well and that reflects in her *Terrarium* designs. She chooses plants with similar growth habits, colors, shapes and textures to ensure survival as well as a beautiful landscape.

Landscaping a *Terrarium* is as important as the plants. She adds rocks, sand and cork. She creates elevations and meticulously crafts an incredible tiny geo-sphere. With her background caring for the plants in the family greenhouse, it's no wonder she excels at *Terrariums*.

Place rocks for drainage in bottom first, then add soil. (Cork can be added to create two levels). Plant your vegetation; add tiny clay pot steps, gravel, sand and maybe a figurine or two... Voila! She makes it look so simple. **Watch the video at: uBloom.com/Terrarriums**

FOLIAGE
3 - 5 Small Terrarium Plants

AND...
Glass Container
Rocks, Gravel and Sand
Broken Clay Pots and Cork

Growing Flowers to Arrange

HISTORY

It was a different time when my grandparents and great grandparents ran our greenhouses and flower shop. They had to grow ALL the flowers they sold. Flower production wasn't worldwide and air-transportation had barely been invented. This meant they were obliged to produce flower crops that were meaningful, long-lasting and available in a wide variety of colors and textures.

My great grandparents, Charles and Katie Green, grew *Carnations*, *Roses*, *Chrysanthemums* (as shown in the picture above), *Tulips*, *Freesia*, *Palms*, Violets, *Stephanotis* and *Gardenias* in the greenhouses. *Delphinium*, *Gladiolus*, *Peonies*, *Sunflowers* and other field crops grew outside.

Crops that provided line, mass, and form flowers were chosen, respectively, for the arrangements that could then be created. The greenhouses provided year round production, but it was still a challenge to get certain flowers in bloom in time for the appropriate holidays (*Easter Lilies* and *Poinsettias* for example).

LOCAL RESOURCES

Fast forward to today – California's unique micro-climates allow for year round production of "American Grown Flowers" that are distributed all across the U.S.A. There are also incredible localized growers for fresh flowers and foliage at seasonal Farmer's Markets countrywide.

The difference in climate throughout the USA provides unique and extra special local flowers. For example, *Tulips* and *Peonies* perform better in zones that get winter weather, while *Magnolia Trees* perform better in Southern regions. Visit your Local Independent Nursery or Garden Center for advice on the flowers, foliage, trees and shrubs that thrive in your zone.

 TIP Cut flowers from the garden early in the morning, before the heat of the day. Bring a bucket of water treated with flower food. Cut and place the flowers or foliage into water immediately!

GARDENING

Growing flowers in your garden is rewarding but it takes time and bit of planning. Certain flowers perform better, last longer and are better suited for Flower Arranging. Here's a list of excellent flowers and foliage you can grow (for arranging) in your own garden:

Line: *Gladiolus, Delphinium, Stock, Larkspur, Apple Blossoms, Veronika, Forsythia, Liatris*

Mass: *Rose, Sunflower, Peony, Magnolia, Ranunculas, Zinnia, Dahlias*

Form: *Tulip, Iris, Daffodil, Lily, Lilac, Tulip Tree, Black Eyed Susan, Rudbeckia*

Accent: *Solidago, Yarrow, Babies Breath, Red Bud, Lavender*

Foliage: *Hosta, Viburnum, Ivy, Red Bud, Cotinus, Rosemary, Dill, Basil*

IDEA Bring Flowers! Flowers that you grew, cut and arranged yourself are a meaningful gift. When buying flowers for yourself, buy an additional bunch for a friend or family member. Flowers are made for sharing!

IDEA Just Chill! After cutting flowers and placing in flower food water, allow them to take up water for 1-3 hours, then place them into a refrigerator or cooler for 3-4 hours to harden off stems. This process allows your flowers to last longer.

HINT Many flowers are edible, so growing these flowers allows you to grow them chemical-free, so they can be used in recipes, or as a plate garnish. Read labels and research each plant you believe may be edible to ensure that it is.

Fun with Submerged Flowers

There's an appeal with submerged flowers that's pleasing to the eye; perhaps it's the magnifying effect when they are underwater. Personally, I'm fascinated by the tiny bubbles caused by the transpiration process that form on the petals of the flowers.

This project is a perfect solution for creating elegant centerpieces on a budget with only one or two blossoms. The use of apothecary type jars gives submerged flowers a "cabinet of curiosities" specimen appearance. Adding a submersible LED light device enhances the dramatic effect.

Fact: flowers float! Using a metal flower frog or pin holder is the key to your success with submerged flowers. Place the stem of the flower into the pin holder to provide the weight to hold the flower underwater. The pin holder can be concealed with river rocks, decorative gravel or sea glass.

Arrange the flowers into the pin holder then place gently into the vase. Fill in around the pin holder with decorative stone, place the vase where it will be displayed, then fill it with water.

TIP **Pour water slowly** along the side of the vase, not on top of the flower. The motion of the water can dislodge the flower from the pin holder.

TIP **Moving a vase full of water is tricky.** Use a turkey baster to remove several inches of water before moving.

FLOWERS
Choose a Favorite Flower or Two

FOLIAGE
A Single Leaf or Fern Frond

AND...
Glass Vase
Metal Based Flower Frog
Decorative Stones

HINT Flowers underwater degrade quickly. Create your submerged flowers the day of your event. Typically the water will start to cloud rapidly after about 18 hours.

Fun with Pin Cushion Protea

The unique ways nature has adapted to its surroundings are part of the fun of flowers. *Pin Cushion Protea* is an example of one of Mother Nature's masterpieces. *Pin Cushions* have an interesting "alien" quality that makes it difficult for some to believe it's actually a flower. (Note: Technically *Pin Cushions* aren't *Protea* but rather "*Leucospermum*," a similar type of species.)

As the *Pin Cushion* flower opens, the pin-like stamens release from the fibrous center. They literally spring out so the flower begins to resemble your grandmother's pincushion she used when sewing.

Pin Cushions come in a wide variety of colors and styles; sometimes they resemble sea urchins or coral. This naturally leads us to design a "fish bowl" flower arrangement with an "under the sea" look.

Begin with a metal "pin holder" (also known as a flower frog or kenzan). It is a time honored and eco-conscious way to keep flowers in place in an arrangement.

Place the heavy metal pin holder inside the bubble bowl. Secure the holder to the bottom of the bowl with florist clay. Add your flowers. Conceal the pin holder with

TIP Be Careful! Pin Holders are very sharp; use caution and supervise children. Cut the woody stem of the *Pin Cushion Protea* at 45-degree angle with your florist knife or by-pass cutter to allow easier insertion into the pin holder.

FLOWERS
2 Red Pin Cushion (Tango)
2 Orange Pin Cushion (Succession)
3 Yellow Pin Cushion (Erubescens)
2 "Pine Cone" Leucadendron (Terenifolia)

FOLIAGE
3 Equisetum (Horse Tail Reed)
5 Foxtail Fern
2 Monkey Tail (Fiddlehead Fern)

AND...
20" Bubble Bowl
Pin Holder (Flower Frog)
River Rocks
LED Lighted Disc (Optional)

Flower Friends

MEL RESENDIZ
Protea Farmer
Resendiz Brothers, Fallbrook CA

Mel creates flower magic in the beautiful region of Fallbrook, California. Everyone meeting Mel quickly recognizes that he is an amazing flower farmer. Wander through his fields, amidst butterflies, hummingbirds, gorgeous blooms and you're transported "that much closer to heaven."

Mel has dedicated his life (and flower farm) to growing *Protea, Leucospermum, Leucodendron, Banksia, Grevillea, Wax Flower* and *Kangaroo Paws*. These flower varieties (none of which are native to California) have been introduced by hand, plant-by-plant by Mel himself to the vertical, mountainous micro-climate of Southern California.

Mel's quick wit and passion for flowers are infectious. He's a true joy to be around. You'll see his flowers in this book, at my events and on uBloom.com. Mel's the "Protea Man" and a one-of-kind California flower farmer.

Watch the video at: uBloom.com/ResendizBrothers

with river rocks. Then place the bubble bowl on a LED lighted disc. This creates a fun effect that looks fabulous in low lighting or nighttime events.

Fun flower designs can transport us to different worlds; use your imagination and Mother Nature's creative blossoms to theme your next arrangement.

IDEA Fill the bubble bowl to the top with water. This magnifies the flowers and enhances the "under the sea" theme. Warning: A bubble bowl full of water is very heavy. Use caution and always move bubble bowls with both hands from the bottom. NEVER pick it up from the edge of the bowl.

IDEA Scale it down. This arrangement was created in a large 20" bubble bowl; a similar effect can be created with any size bubble bowl and fewer flowers.

HINT Look for "flower frogs" at antique stores, swap meets or garage/estate sales. It's a great way to reuse/recycle. Plus many original "flower frogs" were made in the USA.

Fun with Pin Cushion Protea

Fun with Calla Lilies

Calla Lilies are unique in their botanical makeup, which makes them quite popular. *Callas* also have high moisture content, therefore allowing them to last longer. *Callas* have extremely rigid stems, which can be difficult to work with, unless you follow the secret tips below.

Wrapping *Calla Lilies* around the inside of a bubble bowl may seem like a time-consuming task but fear not... fun flower lover.

TIP Skin the *Lily*! Using your flower design knife, grab the edge of the *Calla* stem skin at the base of the stem. Then pull the skin away in a small strip all the way up the stem, to the bloom.

This trick releases the tension of the *Calla* stem so that it is extremely bendable and pliable. I placed fresh (very pliable) *Curly Willow* branches into the bubble bowl first; then I added my *Calla Lilies* and a *Tulip* or two. A large tropical leaf or river rocks are other great elements you can add to your bubble bowl arrangement. Add the *Calla Lily* stems after skinning and ensure that the stem end falls into the water base of the bubble bowl.

By curving the stems over, under, around and through, you can create a fun centerpiece inside a bubble bowl. It takes only minutes, but looks like it took hours.

Watch the video at: uBloom.com/CallaLily

 HINT Illuminate your arrangement for a dramatic effect by adding a waterproof string of LED lights into the bubble bowl.

FLOWERS
10 Stems of Calla Lilies
3 White Tulips

FOLIAGE
2 Curly Willow Branches

AND...
12" Bubble Bowl
String of Waterproof LED Lights

Fun with
Rose Lilies

Transport yourself to the land of make-believe with enchanting *Rose Lilies*. Its fragrance is similar to that of the *"Stargazer" Lily*, with the unexpected resemblance of a *Rose*.

    Begin by cutting the blossoms off the burgundy *Carnations* and the *Rose Lilies*. Use the stems to create the base of a topiary form. (Note: In an effort to repurpose, I found a metal container at a garage sale, gave it a coat of red paint, rendering it perfect for this project).

    Arrange the stems into a full block of saturated flower foam placed into container. Start from the middle of the arrangement and continue in a circle toward the outside of the container. This will form a stable "stem" for your topiary.

    After the "stem base" is complete, place a half block of saturated flower foam on top of the stems and press it into place. I wrapped this block of foam with waterproof tape to hold it together, as there are a number of insertions into the foam. Next, add the *Rose Lilies*. (Note: This variety is pollen-free, so you won't need to worry about pollen dust). Be sure to use the buds as well. The *Rose Lily* buds will open over time with the water supply, so you'll have a "second wave" of flowers in the topiary topper.

FLOWERS
25 Burgundy Carnations
5 Stems of Rose Lilies
10 Stems "Sorbonne" Orchid Lilies

AND...
1 Block of Flower Foam
Metal Container painted Red
Waterproof Tape

TIP When using "reclaimed" flower stems as a structure for a topiary form, be sure to place the stems deep into the foam; preferably to the bottom of the container. This adds additional strength and stability to the overall arrangement.

I "based" the container (around the stem) with long-lasting burgundy *Carnations*. "Basing" means to cover the foam completely with just the *Carnation* flower heads. This will provide a wonderful color impact when combined with the red metal container.

HINT **"Reclaimed" stems still need water**, so be sure to place the stems root end down and bud end up. This allows the stems to continue to take up water. If it is done the opposite way, the stem will not absorb the water.

IDEA **Water to the top!** Because the top of the topiary has limited water supply, flower food water can be added to the flower foam top with a turkey baster!

Watch the video at: uBloom.com/RoseLily

HINT Utilize any kind of stem or branch to create the stem of your topiary form. I used the stems from the flowers in the arrangement; however, you could use *Pussy Willows*, *Cattails*, or any type of sturdy stem or branch.

FAVORITE FLOWERS
ROSE LILY

"The *Rose Lily* combines two flowers into one, a *Lily* and a *Rose*. *Rose Lilies* are fragrant, pollen-free, and last incredibly long. Talk about a FUN Flower!"
— J Schwanke

A *Lily* flower with double-petals resembling a *Rose*.

Scientific Name: *Rose lily* is the collective term for the unique series of *Lilium* with double petal flowers.

Rose Lilies come in a variety of colors: Nearly White (as pictured) and Shades of Pink to Fuchsia with White Striations.

Rose Lilies are grown in California and part of America's Flowers. Growers include: Green Valley Floral, KB Farms and The Sun Valley Group

The *Rose Lily* is pollen-free and lightly scented with a very long-lasting vase life.

For more information visit: www.roselily.com

Fun with Flowers

Fun with Emoticon Mums

The iconic "smiley face" *Mum* was very popular in the 70's and one of the first professional flower arrangements I learned to create. We would place a yellow *"Football" Mum* into a vase with a stem or two of fern (*Leather Leaf*). Then we glued a "Smiley Face" to the "face" of the *Chrysanthemum* using black pipe cleaners.

With the popularity of emoticons in today's computer age, we can create a similar arrangement using emoticons that can evoke a variety of feelings. Colons, asterisks, parenthesis, letters and symbols can be combined to create icons to symbolize our moods!

Use black pipe cleaners and a low temperature glue gun to form popular emoticons. Attach them to the face of yellow standard *Mums*; thus, modernizing the 70's "smiley face" into present day emoticons.

You'll also notice a special emoticon from one of my favorite uBloom friends. Tanti Lina is an amazing event designer and talented flower artist in Philadelphia, who always signs her emails with her personal emoticon (^_____^). It was a fitting a tribute to include her emoticon in this project.

 HINT I'm an extreme advocate of cold adhesive for flowers... however when gluing pipe cleaners to the faces of *Chrysanthemums*, I do enlist my low temp glue gun. It's lower temperature glue is less harmful to the flowers... and it adheres well to the pipe cleaners and causes less mess!

FLOWERS
Several Yellow "Football" Chrysanthemums
2 Stems Yellow Kangaroo Paws
2 Stems Solidago
2 Stems Bupleurum
2 Stems Craspedia (Globe) Yarrow
1 Stem Gaillardia

FOLIAGE
3 Stems Melaleuca Diosmifolia

AND...
Appropriate Glass Vase

Fun with Composite Flowers

The concept behind the composite flower is to create a larger, more opulent flower. This is acheived by combining mutiple flowers into a single large blossom, creating something fantastical and eye-catching.

When I was a kid, my grandfather was in charge of creating composite flowers. The "*Glamelias*" made from *Gladiolus* flowers and the "*Duchess Roses*" were popular as wedding flowers. He wired the individual petals by hand and created magnificent fantasy blossoms in the flower shop.

Today... we create composite flowers of all kinds; it's much easier and far less time consuming. I create mine on paper plates. I trim the paper plate to the appropriate size and then use cold flower adhesive. Petals are removed and then glued in concentric circles from the outside to the inside of the paper plate. Upon reaching the center I simply glue one of the flowers to the center to finish the process. In the case of the *Alstroemeria* composite (shown here), I added *"Globe" Yarrow* for a fantasy flower effect.

This method allows just about any flower with multiple petals to be transformed into a composite. *Gladiolus*, *Roses*, *Orchids*, *Calla Lilies*, *Gardenias*, and even delicate *Alstroemeria* can be formed into composite flowers using this gluing technique. No more wiring and taping; I think Grandpa would be amazed, don't you?

Watch the video at: uBloom.com/Composite

FLOWERS
1 Stem of Cymbidium Orchids **OR**
25 Stems of Calla Lilies **OR**
1 Bunch of Alstroemeria
1 Stem Craspedia (Globe) Yarrow

FOLIAGE
5 Black Ti Leaves **OR**
3 Fatsia Leaves **OR**
10 Ivy Leaves

AND...
Paper Plate (with center hole)
2 Pipe Cleaners
1 Tube of Cold Flower Adhesive
 (Rubber Cement will also work)

HINT Place cold adhesive on the back of the flower petal and the paper plate; glue on both surfaces will hold more securely.

Finding Flowers to Arrange

The "Flower World" is full of wonderful resources for flowers and foliage for arranging. I refer to this collective group of resources as "Flower Sellers" because that is what they do... sell flowers!

Today there are several different types of flower sellers. Many large cities have "**Flower Markets**" that offer access to the public at certain hours. San Francisco Flower Market, my personal favorite, is full of flower sellers. Some cater to the professional florists, while others are open to the general public. Flower sellers that cater to the professional florists are known as "Flower Wholesalers" because they broker flowers at special prices for quantity purchases. They also require a tax license or retail operator's certificate with advance notice.

I love Brannan Street in the San Francisco Flower Market! Working with my friends Barbara and Roy at Brannan Street allows me to ship flowers directly from the market, (grown by California Flower Farmers) to my studio in Michigan. This service, provided by flower brokers, allows professional florists access to flowers from California and all over the world.

J will often spend a day at the historic San Francisco Flower Market when visiting the "City by the Bay."

Roy Borodkin (pictured, left) and Barbara Schnur (with J, pictured, right) of Brannan Street, one of my favorite flower sellers located within the Market.

Many **Professional Florists** today cater to the customer interested in creating their own flower arrangements. I love a florist willing to share his or her resources by offering flowers and foliage by the stem for the purpose of flower arranging.

TIP **Creating a relationship** and resource with a local professional can be very advantageous. Visit your local Professional Florist and ask about flowers (and supplies) for arranging.

Grocery Stores are another tremendous resource for flowers and foliage for arranging. Today's markets carry a large quantity of flowers, many locally grown, or seasonally packed in assortments.

Farmers Markets are another of my favorite flower sellers because they offer a magnitude of extremely fresh locally grown flowers. Farmers Markets also provide opportunities to meet the farmer who grows the flowers you are purchasing.

Growing flowers in your own garden for the specific purpose of arranging is another affordable option that will provide extremely fresh flowers and foliage for your projects (more on growing your own flowers on pages 36-37).

TIP On-line resources may seem convenient and very affordable; however, I don't recommend buying flowers on-line unless you already know the vendor well. Quality can be questionable and in many cases, flowers have not been cared for properly.

Fun with
Single Flowers

The simple beauty of a single flower can create an impressive impact. A single blue hued *Hydrangea* blossom with hundreds of florets or a precious *Rose* blossom nurtured and babied into bloom; Flowers are amazing!

I frequently visit antique stores, flea markets and eBay searching for fun flower holders. I look for containers to repurpose that will hold a single bloom beautifully. An apothecary jar filled with aquarium gravel makes the perfect receptacle for a *David Austin® Fragrant English Garden Rose*. A bubble bowl, however, can house a magnificent *Hydrangea* bloom, while filling the space with lavender and blue florets.

For the photo on the left, I found a vintage 50's ceramic ashtray in turquoise. Cutting off the stem of a two-tone *Gerbera Daisy*, I cut a discarded *Rose* stem into two equal pieces and placed them into the cigarette holder to form a resting place for the blossom. The stems cradle the flower and prevent it from lying in the water... helping the flower last for days!

Repurposing comes naturally with shot glasses, which are perfect for a rose or tulip. Cutting the flower short will actually allow for longer vase life. The water has less distance to travel from cut end to the bloom. In addition, the shot glass supports the rose or tulip as they open.

FLOWERS
Any Single Flower

AND...
A Creative Vessel
  (of your choosing)

TIP Support the Flower. Look for vessels that will support flowers, hold the stem upright, and ensure the flower won't fall into the water.

Flower Friends

KIM CARSON
Media Personality
Grand Rapids MI

Kim is a regular guest host on a daily lifestyle show "Take 5 & Company" on the local ABC affiliate. I'm frequently a guest on Take 5, so Kim and I became fast friends. I don't remember how we met. She's just "always been there!" I first heard her DJ on the radio when I moved to Grand Rapids. She has a friendly voice that I welcomed into my home on a daily basis; "the voice" of a DJ that seemed ultra-familiar. I loved surprising her with flowers occasionally when she was on the air and we've hosted many flower events together at the Local Home and Garden Shows.

Not only is Kim a broadcast celebrity (Host of the nationally syndicated Faith, Hope and Love Songs), she's also a published author, poet, and an amazing positive force in the lives of people she touches.

Kim happens to love flowers and boasts a yard full of flowers. She arranges flowers handpicked from her garden, photographs them and shares on social media. Kim lights up any room she walks into and my life is better because we are friends. The fact that we share a passion for flowers just adds to our friendship.

Sell your books at World of Books!

Go to sell.worldofbooks.com and get an instant price quote. We even pay the shipping - see what your old books are worth today!

Inspected By: Marlene_Arevalo

0008919424

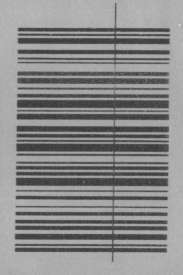

Create a symbolic centerpiece with a single bunch of flowers and 10 shot glasses by arranging a collection of shot glasses into an interesting or romantic shape (a heart for example).

Create a "cocktail" of monumental memories with bar glasses from your home. My cocktail glasses are often used with flowers in my home. (Highballs make great vases, brandy snifters are classic single bloom holders and a martini glass can hold a stemmed Gardenia).

When it comes to repurposing, the options are endless for the perfect vessel for a single flower.

IDEA Look to the Lab! Chemistry vessels are ideal for holding flowers; test tubes, beakers, and other laboratory glassware work great.

Watch the video at:
uBloom.com/SIngleFlowers

HINT Add a Flower Frog. Flower Frogs (especially vintage) can be added to a container to support a single stem, blossom or several stems for a quick arrangement.

Fun with A Single Flower

Fun with Wedding Flowers

Weddings are definitely "ALL about the Flowers." Wedding flowers need to be beautiful, yet long lasting for the ceremony, the photos, and, of course, the reception. The key to longer lasting wedding flowers throughout all of this is a water supply!

I struggled for years with the bouquet holders available in the market until offered an opportunity to create a bouquet for my friends at FloraCraft! I designed the Gala® Bouquet holder to be elegant, comfortable to hold and - most important - easy for arranging flowers! The key is enclosing an entire sphere of foam inside the holder, which results in a larger water supply than other bouquet holders.

The Gala Bouquet holder changed the art of arranging wedding flowers nearly overnight. Cutting and placing the flowers into a sphere of foam makes the arranging process easy for anyone. It's perfect for professionals, brides or their friends that want to arrange beautiful wedding flowers!

Give the Gala Bouquet holder a try, (You can thank me later!)
Watch the video at: uBloom.com/WeddingFlowers

TIP *Calla* **Twist:** Place *Calla Lily* stems into the bouquet holder at full length then twist the stems around the bouquet and affix with a decorative pin!

Bougainvillea | Wild Rose | Osiana Peach | Tiger Lily | Fresh Green

FLOWERS

1 Antique Hydrangea
8 White Bouvardia
3 Blush Mini Calla Lilies
3 Peach Gerbera Daisies
4 "Esperance Roses"
4 "Anna" Roses
4 Peach Roses
6 Hot Pink Carnations

AND...

Large Gala Bouquet Holder
Pink Petunia "Just for Flowers"
Orange & Pink Ribbon
Bamboo Skewer
Decorative Pins

 HINT Stick the Ribbon: Using the flat end of a bamboo skewer, place lengths of ribbon into your bouquet by pushing the ribbon directly into the bouquet holder. The foam will grab the ribbon and hold it in place.

Fun with Orchid Garlands

Orchids are among the longest lasting and most durable of flowers. *Orchid* flowers can be handled and manipulated quite easily. That's why they are used to make leis in Hawaii. The *Orchid* flower can last for several days without water. Wedding and event designers capitalize on this attribute so you may have experienced *Orchids* used in elaborate weddings and special events. Because of their durability and long lasting qualities, orchid blossoms are also frequently used in the construction of floats for the *World Famous Tournament of Roses Parade* in Pasadena, California. (However, most of these are usually imported.)

I set a *Manzanita* branch in a container with plaster (available at your local craft store). After it is dry and secure, I concealed wet flower foam in the container with a bunch of *Bear Grass* and arranged stems of *Orchids* into the foam.

I strung individual blooms of *Orchids* into garlands using a needle and string. Create 6-inch garlands with 12-14 blooms that are tied into the branches. Coat the *Orchid* garlands with Chrysal Professional Glory to enhance the lasting quality.

Using *Orchids* in an unexpected way really brings out the "Fun with Flowers!"

FLOWERS
10 Stems Magenta Orchids
10 Stems Pink/White Orchids
70 Pink/White Orchid Blooms
(about 10 or more stems)

FOLIAGE
One Bunch of Bear Grass

AND...
Manzanita Branch
Plaster of Paris
Plastic Bowl
Large Needle & String

HINT Floss your *Orchids*. Dental floss works well as a durable fiber to create orchid garlands.

Fun with
Flowers for Pets

My dogs are part of my family. They are included in celebrations so they need flowers too! Flowers for pets need to be safe, secure and durable.

    I like creating a garland of flowers that can be worn around a pet's neck. The project shown here is much easier than it looks.

    I started with three one-yard lengths of sheer two-inch ribbon and three stems of *Clematis*. Then I tied the end of the three ribbons into a knot and secured the end of the *Clematis* into the knot. Using one stem of *Clematis* and ribbon per chord, I braided the *Clematis* and ribbon together. I measured the neck of my dog Ellie, after completing the braiding. Then I used the free ends to tie the braid into a circle of the length measured.

    These long tendrils of leaves topped with a vibrant *Clematis* blossom are natural garlands. Create a wonderful cascading effect by adding a long *Clematis* stem to an arrangement. The blossoms are long lasting and colorful!

    Ellie loves wearing flowers… who can blame her!

    I was introduced to *Clematis* as a cut flower by my friends at Roseville Farms in Apopka, Florida (one of the largest commercial *Clematis* growers in the world). Roseville grows *Clematis* plants for nurseries and

FLOWERS
3 Stems of Clematis

AND...
3 One Yard Lengths of Sheer Ribbon

 TIP Safety First: If you need to secure a stem or ribbon, use a pipe cleaner; it's soft and can be trimmed or folded back to reduce sharp points.

greenhouses. They recently added cut stems of *Clematis* (about 36-48 inches long) to their offerings.

The name *Clematis* is derived from Ancient Greek, meaning "climbing vine". Scientists have identified over 297 species of this climbing garden vine. This popular garden flower has been adorning the garden trellises since 1862.

Clematis is also known as the "Queen of the Vines" or "Vase Vine." That explains why it looks so regal whenever it is added to an arrangement.

 HINT Give your garden a go. *Clematis* from your garden can be cut and used in flower arrangements. Cut the stems early in the morning and place into cold, flower nutrient-treated water before arranging.

FAVORITE FLOWERS
CLEMATIS

Clematis flowers typically have 6 colorful petals with a contrasting center that opens to reveal a multitude of stamens. The flowers grow atop a long vine with sporadic leaves.

"*Clematis* Flowers look so fragile, but in reality they are durable, long lasting and come in unique colors that are uncommon in the flower world!"
— J Schwanke

Clematis is a member of the *Ranunculaceae* (*Buttercup*) family.

Clematis has a unique fibrous stem (rather than vascular) which means the stem can actually be bent and still take up water.

The particularly fuzzy centered prominent seed heads are referred to as "Old Man's Beard."

Clematis comes in a wide variety of colors, Purple, Lavender, Blue, Red, Burgundy, Pink, White and bi-colors.

Watch the video at: uBloom.com/RosevilleFarms

Fun with Clematis

Fun with
Mercury Glass

Mercury Glass has always fascinated me. It holds a vintage appeal and is perfect for a party! Gazing globes were sold at our family flower shop. Large mercury glass yard ornaments were hot sellers.

Vintage mercury glass is rare however; many vintage vessel shapes are being reproduced with mercury glass effects! The cube and the votive cups pictured here are actually new pieces with a vintage feel. Hanging votives are the perfect way to suspend candlelight above the arrangement.

I sprayed a branch of *Curly Willow* with Design Master® Super Silver paint and placed it into the flower foam inside the container. I hung the votives from the branch and accented the branch with silver flat wire. What a beautiful sight.

Our mini color palette accents Silver... and this selection of hot pink California Grown Flowers provides the perfect "pop" for party flowers. *Gerbera Daisies, Star-gazer Lilies* and *"Quincy" Spray Roses* from Eufloria Flowers pair perfectly with the mercury glass! (The *Silver Tree Leucadendron* used is naturally silver. That's how it grows.)

Raspberry   Fuchsia

IDEA **Silver Linings!** Use a Silver permanent marker on a *Lily* or *Gerbera* petal to create fun "mercury" accents on the flowers, or draw a monogram on a leaf!

FLOWERS
4 Stems of Star-gazer Lilies
3 Stems of Hot Pink Gerberas
2 Stems of "Quincy" Spray Roses

FOLIAGE
2 Stems of Silver Tree
1 Curly Willow Branch

AND...
Silver Mercury Glass Cube
Hanging Mercury Glass Votives
2 yards of Silver Flat Wire
1 Block of Flower Foam
Super Silver Design Master Paint

HINT Flame-free! For safety use battery operated LED lights inside the mercury glass for brightness and to ensure they won't blow out!

THE SECRETS TO
Longer Lasting Flowers

Expert care and handling procedures allow your flower arrangements to last even longer. Although I've had a lifetime of experience with this, I'm always reading the latest research report on cut flower care. Groundbreaking research has proven that many conventional flower care and handling processes are obsolete. Some are actually bad for your flowers and their longevity.

For longer lasting flowers, follow these easy flower care and handling tips.

PUBLIC ENEMY #1 - BACTERIA

Less Bacteria = Flower Longevity. Here's how to avoid bacteria:

Use ice cold water. By using ice cold water with flower food to hydrate and process any flowers or foliage, you can significantly reduce bacteria growth. Cold water also contains less air than warm water.

Clean your flower buckets, containers, & tools. Cleaning frequently with soap and water (*or better yet Professional Flower Cleaners - I like Chrysal Professional Bucket Cleaner*) helps remove and reduce bacteria growth.

Remove leaves that fall below the water line. Foliage (and flowers) that fall under water create bacteria fast!

A hint especially for Fuzzy-stemmed flowers. *Gerbera Daisies* have fuzzy stems that create bacteria faster when placed in water. CVBn tablets (by Chrysal) help control bacteria levels with "dirty stem" flowers. CVBn tablets are available from reputable flower sellers. *Sunflowers* and *Celosia* will also benefit. Disregard "old wives' tales" about aspirin, pennies, bleach, and soda pop. None actually work.

Flower food contains everything your flowers need. Flower food is scientifically formulated to lengthen flower vase life; always keep a few packets on hand.

Read the flower food directions and measure accurately. It is important to measure as too much or too little flower food is far worse than using none at all.

BEWARE BOTRYTIS

Keep your flower blossoms dry. Botrytis (bacteria) spreads rapidly on wet surfaces, especially wet flowers. Botrytis infects and kills flowers fast. Follow these steps to keep Botrytis in check:

Watch out! Don't purchase flowers that show signs of Botrytis (see picture, at right).

Never immerse flower heads in water. Water in or on flower blooms creates the perfect breeding ground for Botrytis.

Wash your hands. If you remove Botrytis petals or blossoms, wash your hands (or tools) before touching other flowers.

Keep it clean! Keep your containers, tools and work surfaces clean to prevent Botrytis.

TOOLS & PROCEDURES

Use the right tools. Cut your flowers with a sharp knife or by-pass cutters (pruner) at a 45 degree angle and place immediately into ice cold flower food treated water (more about tools on pages 88-89).

No underwater cutting! There's no evidence that cutting flowers underwater makes them last longer; frankly, it's dangerous and difficult. Keep your eye on the knife, cutting where you can see clearly and safely.

DON'T SWEAT IT

Use an Anti-Transpirant on your completed flower arrangements. I swear by Chrysal Professional Glory, it's an Anti-Transpirant spray that helps flowers last longer! Spray your flowers front and back — shaking off the excess. As they dry, blossoms won't be able to transpire moisture as quickly through the petals.

Anti-Transpirant sprays are ideal for wedding or event flowers and flowers to wear, especially for warm locations or hot weather.

Anti-Transpirant sprays also deter Botrytis growth, so it's OK to spray it on all flowers!

 TIP Treat your Flowers like Vegetables. Use cold water to clean and prep them. Keep them cool and keep an eye out for "rotten spots or yellow leaves." Bright colors and dark green leaves are signs of freshness.

Fun with Orchid Stems

Mother Nature arranges *Orchid* blossoms perfectly on the stem. They are also long-lasting and easy to arrange. Arranging *Orchids* by the stem allows you to create contemporary designs quickly and easily.

The rectangle cube pictured here is definitely one of my favorite vases because of its versatility. It's a big vase; however, it comes in smaller sizes. A rectangle vase of any proportion is a good investment for the flower arranger.

I used the decorative river rocks in this arrangement to hold the stems in place. It's a "mechanic" we favored long before flower foam. I also added a few stems of *Curly Willow* into the vase before any flowers to help hold flowers in place. We call this technique "Hana-kubari" (a lesson from my Ikebana flower arranging studies in Japan in the 70's).

I simply layer the *Orchid* stems; longest go in first, extending out one end of the vase at an angle. I also included *Bear Grass* and *Flax* foliage between several types of *Orchid* stems. The finished arrangement is impressive both under water and above. Large or small, this arrangement is fast and easy.

FLOWERS
5 Stems Oncidium Orchids
2 Stems Brown Cymbidium Orchids
10 Stems Mokara Orchids

FOLIAGE
1 Bunch Bear Grass
5 Stems Brown Flax
5 Stems Curly Willow Branches

AND...
Large 15" Rectangle Vase
2 Bags of Assorted River Rocks

IDEA Scale it down! For a smaller arrangement, use a smaller vase. *Curly Willow* with 10 stems of *Dendrobium Orchids*, which are not as large as *Cymbidiums*, work well.

Fun with
Iris and Ginger

At the family greenhouse property, we grew *Bearded Iris*. I remember *Bearded Iris* with lots of long thin foliage; the corms (tuberous roots) were visible where the plant met the ground. This recollection was my inspiration for this project.

Bearded Iris

Fill a metal window box type container with soaked flower foam, then insert bamboo skewers into *Ginger Root* (purchased at the grocery store). Place the *Ginger Roots* into the foam so they're "climbing" over the edge of the window box; as *Iris* corms might do.

I added *Mushrooms* (they were placed on toothpicks and then into the foam) along with *Foxtail Fern* and *Variegated Flax* leaves. The foliage, *Ginger* and *Mushrooms* "create" the *Iris* bed. Since *Bearded Iris* have only seasonal availability, I added several bunches of USA Grown *"Telstar" Iris* (available nearly year round) from Sun Valley Flower Farm.

Taking creative license with an arrangement is fun. This arrangement represents the way I think about the *Iris* of my childhood; it's interpretive and not necessarily accurate but it enlivens my memory. That's what "Fun with Flowers" is all about!

FLOWERS
20 Stems of "Telstar" Iris

FOLIAGE
10 Stems of Foxtail Fern
10 Stems of Variegated Flax Leaves

AND...
8 Ginger Roots
1 Box of Mushrooms
Bamboo Skewers/Toothpicks
3 Blocks of Flower Foam
Metal Window Box Container

TIP Bend it! Bending the *Flax* leaves at an angle gives a natural appearance to the leaves and makes them look more like Iris leaves.

Fun with Tulips on the Bulb

Tulips are synonymous with Spring. However, *Tulips* grow all over the planet. In fact, Southern Hemisphere *Tulips* come up at the exact opposite time of year from those in the Northern. *Tulips* can also be "forced" to bloom anytime of the year by cooling bulbs and simulating Winter conditions.

My family had bulb caves where we planted pots of *Tulips* and placed them into the cave (in later years we placed them in our flower coolers). This is where they maintained a cold temperature for a specified time. Then we would bring the pots of pre-cooled *Tulip* bulbs into the warm sunny greenhouses and in a few weeks, we would have *Tulips*!

Sun Valley Farms in Arcata, California, has perfected this process. Sun Valley combines the perfect soil, climate and temperatures of the region to provide *Tulips* 24-7 to

 TIP Light is right! *Tulips* are phototropic, and the blooms open and close as light changes throughout the day. Stems grow toward light sources. Keep this in mind when arranging your *Tulips*!

FLOWERS
6 Bunches of Soil Grown Tulips on the Bulb (10 Stems per Bunch)
10 Stems Bells of Ireland

FOLIAGE
10 Stems of Seeded Viburnum Foliage

AND...
Italian Style Resin Urn
6 Blocks of Flower Foam

Flower Friends

LANE DEVRIES
Flower Farmer
Sun Valley Group, Arcata CA

Lane DeVries creates "*Tulip* Magic" every day in Arcata, California. I spent a day following him through the intricate, amazing growth process of Sun Valley *Tulips*. (He also grows Iris, Ilex, *Hydrangea*, *Lilies*, *Hyacinth*, *Freesia* and many more varieties.)

Lane chose to raise *Tulips* in Arcata because the average temperature fluctuates just 10 degrees year round, so it's always a perfect environment for raising these beautiful flowers. Lane also discovered that the soil in Humboldt County — organic compost that is rich, dark and full of nutrients — is perfect for *Tulips* to thrive. Sourcing bulbs from around the world, Lane makes the best use of this environment to grow *Tulips* 24-7 from soil to vase.

This man knows how to grow flowers and passionately provides "World Class Flowers" throughout America.

This passion, and more than a share of talent, help Lane grow perfect *Tulips* and so much more!

Watch the video at: uBloom.com/SunValleyArcata

the Flower Seller. Using bulbs from both hemispheres and a cooling process, Sun Valley harvests *Tulips* all year.

When the *Tulips* begin to flower, the bulb and all are removed from the soil. The *Tulips* are then placed inside coolers. The coolers hold them in a form of "suspended animation"... until it's time to sell them... thus allowing Sun Valley to provide American soil grown tulips 24/7.

I built up a pyramid of soaked flower foam in the center of the urn and placed bunches of "*Tulips* on the Bulb" on top. The flower bunches were held in place with wooden stakes (placed through the bunch where they are bundled). I added *Viburnum* foliage and *Bells of Ireland* around the flower bunches, creating this magnificent *Tulip* arrangement.

Watch the videos at:
uBloom.com/TulipBulbs
uBloom.com/TulipTime

IDEA Spring ahead! The bulbs can be planted in your garden after the flowers have expired and you'll have *Tulips* that come up the following Spring!

Fun with Fruit and Flowers

Sometimes an elaborate looking arrangement can be the easiest to create. This design combines three elements, including fruit, into an impressive display. The base is a glazed 12" diameter ceramic pot. I found a bucket that hides inside the ceramic pot and holds several bunches of *Hybrid Delphinium*, standing in flower nutrient water.

The wreath of flowers and fruit is arranged into a saturated flower foam wreath with a 12" in diameter base (the same size as the ceramic pot). I placed woods picks into *Lemons*, using both whole and half *Lemons* and randomly inserted them into the wreath. Spaces in between the *Lemons* were filled with *Bupleurum*, and "Yellow Island" *Roses*.

Place the pot where you want it to be displayed, and then place the bucket of water into the ceramic pot. Place the wreath frame on top of the ceramic urn. (Use florist's clay to hold the wreath in place if you want extra stability). Drop bunches of *Hybrid Delphinium* into the bucket inside the ceramic pot.

Presto! These three combined elements create a stunning flower arrangement fit for a king.

FLOWERS
50 Stems Hybrid Delphinium Light & Dark Blue
25 Stems "Yellow Island" Roses
5 Stems Bupleurum

AND...
2 Dozen Lemons
6" Wood Picks
15" Flower Foam Wreath Frame
Flower Bucket
12" Diameter Ceramic Pot

 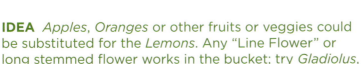

IDEA *Apples*, *Oranges* or other fruits or veggies could be substituted for the *Lemons*. Any "Line Flower" or long stemmed flower works in the bucket; try *Gladiolus*, *Bells of Ireland* or *Liatris*.

Fun with
Vegetables and Flowers

Combining flowers with unexpected items provides fun in so many ways. This Italian-inspired arrangement combines vegetables and flowers to create a stunning display for an Italian dinner with flower-inspired dishes.

    I'm a notorious "foodie." I love to eat. I'm inspired by delicious food and I want my flower arrangements to "stand up" to the incredible food being served. At the same time, vegetables, fruit and flowers naturally go together.

    I love this Italian-inspired resin urn. I stacked 5 soaked flower foam blocks for this arrangement (secured with bamboo stakes and waterproof tape). I selected *Tomatoes* on the vine, *Eggplant*, *Artichokes*, *Broccoli*, *Peppers*, a purple head of *Cabbage*, even *Asparagus*. All of these coordinated with my flowers.

    Artichokes are grown commercially as flowers as well as for eating. The large purple thistle-like blooms highlight this arrangement. Add vegetables by placing them on bamboo skewers and then insert into the flower foam. Use purple and lavender flowers to accent and fill spaces.

    Richard Seaboldt, a long time mentor and legendary flower artist, was the first to inspire me to combine vegetables and flowers. Richard has never feared any combination, boldly designing for state dinners, and extraordinary events for decades.

HINT Place large bulky vegetables first (head of *Cabbage*, *Broccoli*, *Eggplant*) to allow you space to fill in with more delicate flowers and vegetables. This creates a more cohesive arrangement!

FLOWERS
10 Purple Agapanthus
10 Lavender Campanula
4 Burgundy Stemmed Artichokes
3 Artichoke Blossoms
6 Green Hydrangea
10 Cream Hypericum
4 Viburnum Berry Branches
10 Purple Veronika
10 Green Carnations

VEGETABLES
2 Eggplant
2 Broccoli
1 Red Cabbage
1 Broco-flower
2 Stems of Tomatoes

FOLIAGE
10 Burgundy Ti Leaves

AND...
Italian Resin Urn
6 Blocks of Flower Foam
Waterproof Anchor Tape
Wood Picks

Flower Friends

JENNA ARCIDIANCONO
Chef
Amoré Tratorria Italiana, Grand Rapids MI

Jenna and I met when we were asked to join forces for a women's business luncheon for a local bank. Chef Jenna prepared her signature Northern Italian cuisine (the finest I've ever tasted). I created fun flower arrangement ideas for the holidays!

Chef Jenna and her husband Mauricio own Amoré Trattoria (my favorite Italian restaurant, located in Grand Rapids, MI). Jenna began her cooking career by learning first hand from Mauricio's mama in Milan, Italy. Jenna spoke very little Italian, yet they communicated through food preparation... talk about fun!

Jenna and I share our passions. Her vivacious personality is just as incredible as her family recipes. I play second fiddle to Chef Jenna at her monthly cooking classes where she shares her love for cooking. I offer flower arranging tips as she prepares the culinary delights.

I also arrange the flowers for her restaurant. We bring in farm fresh local flowers to complement her "farm to table" seasonal menus. The world's finest Northern Italian dishes paired with fun flowers, now there is a match made in Heaven...

Bon Appétit!

Fresh produce can be an inspiration for flower arranging. I love the combination of textures. Allowing your flowers to co-mingle with other textural elements is natural and will allow the line between food and flowers to blur beautifully.

My friend Chef Jenna created "Rosacello" for this special event. "Rosacello" is a specialized alcoholic drink (adapted from a "Limoncello" recipe) that Chef Jenna made from Roses (Rose petals) instead of lemons. She used *David Austin® Fragrant English Garden Roses* grown organically in my garden. I thought it would be fun to share the recipe to accompany your next flower or vegetable project.

Watch the video at: uBloom.com/VegetablesFlowers

RECIPE
Rosacello di Amoré
1 bottle of Everclear Alcohol (750 ml)
Petals of 10 Dried Organic Roses
6 cups Sugar
8 cups Water

1. Combine the dried rose petals with Everclear.
2. Transfer to a large Ball canning jar. Let it sit for 2 weeks.
3. Make a simple syrup by combining water and sugar. Boil until sugar is dissolved and chill in the refrigerator.
4. After the 2 weeks - strain the petals from alcohol.
5. Mix with the simple syrup to taste.

Yield 2 - 2 1/2 bottles per one bottle of Everclear.

Store in your freezer and serve after dinner! Saluté!

IDEA Put the Flowers Inside! Bell Peppers or Melons can be filled with soaked flower foam and flowers can be arranged directly into the produce!

Fun with Sunflowers

Sunflowers bring joy to my life. I love the way the big, bright yellow petals contrast with the black center. *Sunflowers* grow with the sun. Have you seen pictures of *Sunflower* fields with all the flowers miraculously pointing in the same direction? *Sunflowers* are phototropic and follow the light source across the sky.

I created an armature — a framework for creating an arrangement — out of *Curly Willow* to secure flowers in place inside the vase. I used a large rectangle vase with just a few flowers, so the armature helped me arrange the flowers artfully!

I placed several stems of *Curly Willow* into the vase first. Then I began twisting, curving and attaching the ends to other branches with small pieces of flat gold decorative wire. (Clamping the connection point is easy with the flat wire... see photo). This allowed me create a stable framework into which to place flowers. *Sunflowers* and additional flowers could be added as well if you wish.

Suddenly... "Fun" becomes "Art" and you're the Flower Artist!

TIP Reuse the Framework! Once constructed, an armature can be dried, then used over and over with the same vase.

Watch the video at: uBloom.com/Sunflowers

HINT This time honored construction is ideal for arrangers who prefer to forego the use of flower foam.

FLOWERS
5 Sunflowers
2 Yellow Kangaroo Paws
3 Yellow Pin Cushion Protea
10 Craspedia (Globe) Yarrow

FOLIAGE
5 Aspidistra Leaves
6 Curly Willow Branches

AND...
15" Rectangle Vase
1 Yard of Flat Gold Decorative Wire

The Right
Flower Arranging Tools

Using the right tools… makes every job easier! The same goes for flower arranging. Specific tools make it easier to cut and arrange your flowers; using these tools will also make them last longer. The two go hand in hand.

THE FLORIST KNIFE & PROPER TECHNIQUE

Swiss Army® Locking Blade Knife My favorite flower arranging tool is my Swiss Army Knife. This is not the version packed with all sorts of gadgets and gizmos, but rather a knife designed specifically for flower arranging by Swiss Army. This knife has a blade that can be folded into the handle and when opened "locks" into place (thus the name). This allows you to cut without the worry of the blade folding back; perfect for cutting flowers.

All flowers benefit from being cut with a knife at a 45-degree angle. A sharp knife is your friend and ensures your flowers will last longer. Swiss Army also makes a great sharpener that sharpens your knife with a few quick swipes. For years there were only two choices of handle colors; red and black! Today the colorful handles available are fun and fashionable.

Cutting flowers with a knife must be perfected, but when perfected it's the fastest, easiest way to cut flowers for arranging. Here's a link to a video on uBloom.com that you can watch to show you how to cut flowers with a knife correctly. **Watch the video at:** uBloom.com/CuttingFlowers

OTHER TOOLS

Bunch Cutters This works well for cutting a whole bunch of flowers at one time. Many people use bunch cutters to "process" large quantities of flowers. (By-pass Cutters work too)

By-pass Cutters They are wonderful for thick woody stems (i.e. *Protea* or *Lilac*). They cut through large diameter more easily than with a knife.

Scissors I use scissors for ribbon; some people like the safety factor of scissors rather than a knife to cut stems. However, scissors can crush the vascular system of the flower and prevent it from taking up water (a bunch cutter can do this too).

HINT Skip the Scissors. Cutting flowers with scissors is like cutting a paper straw with scissors. After its cut, it's crushed and compressed, making it harder to take up liquids.

Chrysal Rose Stripper I love my soft plastic rose stripper for removing foliage and thorns, its' soft and gently removes the foliage and just the tips of the thorns. It's perfect for removing foliage that would fall below the water level!

FLOWER BUCKETS & CLEANLINESS

Clean buckets are equally important to longer lasting flowers. I keep a toilet brush around to help scrub my buckets. Anytime a bucket begins to have visible staining, I don't use it for flowers anymore. When you can see the stains, it's no longer a useable bucket.

TIP Keep your tools clean. Flowers hate bacteria and it shortens their life. Keeping your tools clean prevents bacteria from building up on your knife, scissors or bunch cutters. Cutting flowers with dirty tools is definitely not recommended.

Fun with Ombré Colors

Ombré colors are all the rage! Ombré means colors or tones that shade into each other. This gentle movement between colors residing next to another on the color wheel, is easy to achieve with flowers (along with a little special secret).

For this Ombré arrangement that moves from blue to green, I had to address the color aqua (or turquoise). There are very few flowers that truly grow in aqua or turquoise hues. That's where my friend Gretchen Sell at Design Master came in. Gretchen helped develop a line of translucent French spray dyes (called "Just for Flowers") that can gently wash a color and move it from one value to another.

I used the "Peacock" Just for Flowers and gently "air-brushed" the translucent aqua tone over blue *Eryngium*.

I started with my darkest blue flowers, transitioning to lighter blue, then added the "aqua" *Eryngium* and turquoise *Tweedia*, into green *Amaranthus*, *Grasses*, and chartreuse *Viburnum* and *Fugi Chrysanthemums*. I painted a glass rectangle vase with 24k Gold Paint from Design Master to provide an opulent contrast.

The transition is seamless because I address the tints, tones and shades of the color wheel naturally and with "Just for Flowers" (available from Professional Florists or Florist Supply Resources).

FLOWERS
5 Dark Blue Delphinium
5 Veronika
3 Blue Iris
3 Blue Hyacinth
1 Light Blue Hydrangea
3 Light Blue Delphinium
2 Tweedia
2 Eryngium (tinted aqua)
3 Green Upright Amaranthus
1 Green Viburnum
1 Green Fuji Chrysanthemum
2 Green Tea Roses

FOLIAGE
5 Assorted Grasses

AND...
1 Block of Foam
Glass Rectangle Vase
24k Gold Paint
Peacock "Just for Flowers"

Blue Bright | Mineral Blue | Peacock | Spring Green | Prairie Grass

HINT Go Slow! When it comes to color enhancing flowers, it's best to use several light coats of paint, allowing each to dry fully between applications. The results will be softer and more natural.

Fun with Changing Colors

Color is important! Our favorite color can reveal as much about ourselves as our horoscope. Color can also help set the stage for any flower arrangement. Lee Eiseman, my friend and color expert, has written numerous books on how color can affect or enhance our mood.

Sometimes, however, you just can't find flowers in the right color. Being adventurous, creative, and picking up a can of Design Master® Paint can help you create an unexpected color theme with all sorts of flowers.

This metal pail is filled with an assortment of unique garden flowers in a bright, summery color palette inspired by one of my favorite flowers, *Tree Peonies*. Thanks to Design Master, I used Coral Bright and Fuchsia Bright to enhance some of the flowers in this arrangement in a natural and unexpected way.

Snowball Viburnum is gently shadowed with Fuchsia Bright, and a *"Gerando" Gerbera Daisy* layered with Coral Bright, heavier to the outside and back. The flowers look natural yet the color is unexpected and pairs with other vibrant colors from the garden.

Layering Coral Bright over "golden yellows" provides a unique coral tone. Washes of intense color layered on white flowers create a natural blush,

FLOWERS
3 Fuchsia Tree Peonies
3 Snowball Viburnum
3 Red "Gerando" Gerbera Daisies
3 Yellow "Gerando" Gerbera Daisies
5 Scabiosa
6 Red Astilbe
3 Pink Carnations
3 Variegated Pink/White Carnations
5 Orange Gomphrena
4 Pink Cottage Yarrow
4 Yarrow
5 "Denim Star" Eufloria Spray Roses
5 China Asters

FOLIAGE
5 Cotinus

AND...
Metal Pail
Block of Flower Foam
Design Master Coral Bright Paint
Design Master Fuchsia Bright Paint

 TIP Shadow effect. Using a strong color you can lightly shade one side or edges of a blossom in a complementary tone, providing an unexpected, yet natural color enhancement.

similar to what we see in *PeeGee Hydrangea* in the Fall. Changing colors is about the blending process, it's like "make-up" for flowers!

Most of the flowers in this bouquet are naturally bright. Enhancing the more subdued colors with bright tints allows us to keep the entire collection vibrant and eye-catching. Design Master Paints are designed specifically for flowers and allow me to blend bright colors naturally. Done artfully and carefully... even Mother Nature might not suspect.

TIP Cut *Tree Peonies* before they are completely open - buds will open in an arrangement. Also, early morning is the best time to cut *Peonies*, before the heat of the day.

FAVORITE FLOWERS
Tree Peony

The traditional flower symbol for China. Large ornamental flowers are often fragrant with different petal formations that surround a seeded center.

"A single *Tree Peony* bloom is an arrangement in itself; refined foliage, vibrant petals surround a jewel-like center! It is opulent, elegant and beautiful!" — J Schwanke

Mischievous Nymphs are said to hide in the petals of the *Peony*, giving it the meaning of "bashfulness" in the language of flowers.

Tree Peonies come in several colors: a variety of Pinks, Peaches, Fuchsia, Burgundy, Coral (as pictured) White, and Yellow.

Scientific Name: *Paeonia* (named after Paeon, whom Zeus turned into a flower to save him from the wrath of "Asclepius the Greek God of Medicine & Healing").

Fun with Tree Peony

Fun with Complementary Colors

Complementary colors are unique pairs of colors that reinforce each other to create exciting contrasts. Using this striking visual opposition in our flower arrangements will enhance emotions... in the same way the bright orange leaves of a *Maple* tree in the fall contrast against the crisp, blue Autumn sky.

I arranged "groupings" of orange flowers between the blue "patches" of color to create this look. Soil grown *Tulips*, *Calendula* (which when grown organically is "edible"), *"Milva" Roses*, and *Banksia Protea* (also known as *"Bottle Brush" Protea*) are strategically placed in saturated flower foam inside this blue urn.

Working with different color combinations in flower arrangements helps you experience the emotional partnership between color and flowers. Take a moment to play with the color combinations and see which one complements your style.

The flowers in this arrangement are all locally grown in the USA.

TIP Experts in this field tell us that people who like orange are creative and adventurous. Blue lovers are dependable, popular and traditional. The art of complementary colors has the potential to create a beautiful, attention-grabbing flower arrangement. What's your favorite color?

FLOWERS
2 Blue/Purple Hydrangea
5 Blue Hybrid Delphinium
5 Dusty Miller
10 Orange Tulips
5 "Milva" Orange Roses
5 Tweedia
5 Calendula
1 Banksia Protea

FOLIAGE
5 Dusty Miller

AND...
Urn painted Blue
1/3 Block of Flower Foam
Waterproof Tape

Fun with
Rainbow Colors & Flowers

Rainbows are magical. They appear after a thunderstorm in that instant when the sun bursts through the clouds... colors line up in a chromatic fashion arching across a rain drenched landscape. And let's not forget the proverbial "pot of gold" at the end of every rainbow!

Naturally, I'm crazy about dyed flowers too. The method itself is amazing; cutting a flower and placing into a concentrated dye mixture... after about 20 minutes... presto... the flower is coloring itself from the inside. It's a favorite experiment in elementary school science class.

For this arrangement, I used an assortment of "color-enhanced" *Chrysanthemums* from Esprit Miami. *Fugi Mums* and *Daisy Pompons* in hot colors. They are are arranged into flower foam that has been taped into a clear dish and sits atop the ginger jar filled with Deco Beads®.

Deco Beads are fun water storing beads that come in a wide variety of colors. They are the creation of my friend, Dave Czehut... and I love designing with them. Here I layered different colors of Deco Beads, starting with purple, then blue, aqua, green, yellow, orange and finally red at the very top. Because the Deco Beads reflect light, they shimmer like jewels and blend whimsically from color to color. You're creating your own rainbow... with Deco Beads and flowers.

Who needs a pot of gold? We're having "Fun with Flowers!"
Watch the video at: uBloom.com/RainbowColors

FLOWERS

12 Stems Dyed Fugi Mums in Blue, Green and Hot Pink

15 Stems Dyed Daisy Pompons in Red, Orange and Purple

AND...

1/2 Block of Flower Foam
6" Clear Design Tray
Water Proof Anchor Tape
Ginger Jar
Deco Beads in Purple, Blue, Aqua, Green, Yellow, Orange and Red

HINT Light it up! Add a submersible LED lighting unit to your Deco Beads to give them an illuminating effect.

Fun with
Black Roses

Black Roses enjoy a mysterious aura. People ask for *Black Roses*, teenagers commonly want a *Black Rose* and on occasion even a bride will request *Black Roses*. While nature does not provide a true *Black Rose*... my friends Chris and Kelle at Esprit Miami have come up with a *Black Rose* that looks natural.

By taking a *Red Rose* and color enhancing it with concentrated navy blue dye... they developed this mystical *Black Rose*. You'll notice the rose is actually very deep dark red. It's perfect for a dramatic contemporary arrangement or gothic-styled event. *Black Roses* will get lots of attention.

I created a sphere of *Black Roses* to set on a black dish with black stones as part of this table arrangement. Then I placed another sphere of *Black Roses* atop a black pilsner vase. I didn't fill in that sphere completely so I could add *Contorted Willow*; a few *Black Succulents*, *Agonis* and some black *Calla Lilies*! I added a few black *Emerald Leaves* for dramatic effect. However, the star of this arrangement is the *Black Rose*!

HINT Bigger! When creating a sphere of flowers, the size of the foam sphere will increase about 1-3 inches in diameter as you add the flowers, so keep that in mind when planning your finished project.

FLOWERS
75 Stems of Black Roses
10 Stems of Black Calla Lilies
5 Black Succulents

FOLIAGE
6 Stems of Agonis
3 Black Emerald Leaves
2 Stems of Contorted Willow

AND...
Large Black Pilsner Vase
Black Glass Tray
Black River Rocks
2 Soaked 6" Flower Foam Spheres

TIP *Black Roses* are created using highly concentrated dyes, be sure to protect your work and display surfaces. Flower dyes are permanent and can stain easily!

IDEAS ON
WORKING WITH COLOR

In my opinion, color is the most important element of Flower Design. Choosing the right colors and combinations will transform a simple flower arrangement into an eye-catching work of art.

THE POWER OF COLOR

Colors also affect our moods. Certain colors can change the way we feel. Color is truly that powerful. It's true! Science has confirmed it. Making the right color choices will provide hours of continuous enjoyment or set the mood for a romantic evening. It can even cause us to feel more calm and relaxed.

I love color! Many times I use a combination of ribbon and flowers to help achieve the perfect ratio or feeling for my arrangements. The ribbon provides a nice transitional element from one color to another.

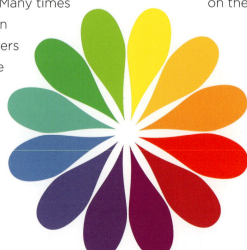

SETTING THE TONE

Choosing the right colors for your flower arrangement will allow you to set the mood for a celebration, party or event. It's important to know how different color combinations can affect your mood. Some examples:

Monochromatic (tints, tones and shades of a single color) – Provide a calming effect. Monochromatic colors are classic and evoke a Zen-like feeling or atmosphere.

Analogous (neighbor colors – side by side on the color wheel) – Create a friendly effect, providing a safe feeling. Analogous colors also can be romantic.

Complementary (opposite colors on the color wheel) – are bold and dynamic. They grab attention and create excitement.

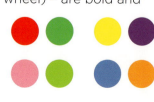

COLOR HOROSCOPES

My friend Lee Eiseman, Director of the Eiseman Center for Color Information and Training, shares the unique ways that certain colors can affect one's mood. Here are some quick "Color Horoscopes" that may offer insights to your favorite colors or how to use them to evoke feelings with your flower arrangements:

- **Yellow:** Positive – Optimistic
- **Peach:** Friendly – Charming
- **Orange:** Creative – Adventurous
- **Red**: Powerful – Seductive
- **Pink:** Innocent – Demure
- **Lavender:** Sentimental – Refined
- **Purple:** Royal – Spiritual
- **Blue:** Dependable – Gentle
- **Aqua:** Tranquil – Calm
- **Chartreuse:** Bubbly – Dynamic
- **Green:** Loyal – Healthy
- **Brown:** Safe – Earthy
- **Black:** Sophisticated – Worldly
- **Grey:** Neutral – Conservative
- **White:** Pure – Neat

IDEA Climate Control. Using exclusively warm or cool colors will allow your flower arrangement to "Heat up" or "Cool down" a party or event.

HINT Primary Colors (yellow, red and blue) when used in combination are perceived as basic and elementary. Secondary Colors (purple, orange and green) when combined create upscale and elegant effects.

 TIP Adding a length of ribbon to an arrangement will enhance the color scheme and add an interesting texture to your flower arrangement.

Fun with Flowers

Fun with Roses

Roses hold a mystical power like no other flower. Virtually everyone loves them. More than 20 years ago, I discovered a very special *Rose* farm (Eufloria Flowers in Nipomo, CA) that grew incredible *Roses* in boutique colors that open perfectly. I decided then and there that Eufloria *Roses* were the "Prettiest Roses on the Planet!"

Fast forward to now. *Eufloria Roses* continue to amaze and delight florists, brides, even farmer's market visitors. Anyone who comes in contact with these amazing *Roses* will most certainly "fall under their spell."

I filled an oversized coffee cup with *Eufloria Roses*, *Hybrid Tea Roses*, *Spray Roses* and a touch of beautiful ribbon. The colors of the *Roses* were picked to coordinate with the cup and saucer. These *Roses* are truly exquisite. They last longer than roses shipped from locations around the world because they are grown right here in the USA.

You'll also appreciate the unusual variety of colors, Lemon, Gold, Mango, Lime, Peach, and even striped. Thanks to *Eufloria Roses*, each *Rose* variety is selected for its growing performance and is perfectly suited for flower arranging.

HINT Look local! Farmers' Markets throughout the country feature flowers that are locally grown. These local treasures will last longer and your purchase supports your community and neighbors.

FLOWERS

1 Yellow Island Rose
2 Miva Roses
1 Naranga Rose
2 Suela Roses
1 Super Green Rose
1 Jazzabell Spray Rose
1 Kelly Spray Rose
1 Yellow Babe Spray Rose
1 Fire Flash Spray Rose

AND...

Oversized Teacup and Saucer
2 Feet Narrow Sheer Orange Ribbon
2 Feet Wide Sheer Yellow Ribbon
1/3 Block of Flower Foam

Flower Friends

LILY GARCIA
Flower Farmer
Eufloria Flowers, Nipomo CA

Lily is the lady behind the prettiest *Roses* on the planet. She is quiet and unassuming, yet her passion for *Roses* is undeniable. I met Lily on a visit to Eufloria Flowers in Nipomo, CA.

Lily not only raises *Roses*, she nurtures the entire Eufloria Flower Farm Family. She quietly observes, teaches and communicates with everyone that comes in contact with the *Roses*. I've watched her plant new *Rose* varieties with care. I've seen her 'pinch' buds and 'bend' stems to encourage better production and larger blossoms. Her watchful eye and nurturing touch is nothing short of "flower magic." Lily's talent and passion shows, because she knows *Roses*. That knowledge benefits everyone who comes in contact with *Eufloria Roses*.

I've traveled to Amsterdam with Andy and Chad from Eufloria to review and select new varieties of *Roses*. This process included samples that would be sent back to Lily so she could plant, test and review each variety in their California coastal greenhouse. She has to ensure the *Rose* would "live up to the Eufloria" reputation.

Lily is "one of a kind," just like a *Eufloria Rose*... enriching our lives, quietly, beautifully and without reservation.

Watch the video at: uBloom.com/EufloriaFlowers

Many varieties of *Eufloria Roses* are fragrant. I love *"Sweet Moments"* and *"Anuhea,"* both exclusive to Eufloria. They smell like traditional *Roses* and remind me of the roses that grew in our family greenhouses.

A single *"Polar Star" Rose* can reside in a glass bowl. It is a fragrant, brilliant white rose about the size of grapefruit. *Roses* are meant to open to display their inner beauty. Many varieties today are bred to be big while remaining "tight" during travel for long distances. They will also withstand being stored in boxes for extended periods. *Eufloria Roses* open, and do so exquisitely. In this photo, three *"Cool Water" Roses* open dramatically in three small containers. Suddenly, three award-winning *Eufloria Roses* become a remarkable centerpiece.

Truly, *Eufloria Roses* are the prettiest *Roses* you may ever encounter. They are grown in the USA; they are colorful, fragrant and long lasting. Does it get any better? "Surrender to the *Eufloria Roses*!"

HINT Skip tight buds! Choose *Roses* that are beginning to open. *Roses* cut too TIGHT may never open; while an opening *Rose* will continue to bloom. Then you'll enjoy the full experience.

Fun with Apsidistra Leaves

Aspidistra leaves are a favorite foliage of mine. I like the green color, texture and dramatic size of the leaf. Most of all, I like the versatility and durability of this Florida Foliage.

Central Florida, specifically Pierson, is the Fern Capital of the World. Much of the "World's Finest Foliage" is grown there, by passionate, dedicated USA Foliage Farmers. *Aspidistra* is one of those "World Class Florida Foliage" varieties.

The strength and durability of these leaves opens up the possibility of woven shapes. I first learned this technique from a street vendor who was selling "*Aspidistra Roses*" and other woven foliage products. Now that I've mastered the skills, I've used these "*Roses*" in arrangements, as wedding bouquets, in funeral tributes and even as Christmas tree decorations.

The "*Roses*" are easy to construct. 10 *Aspidistra* leaves create a 7-8" flower. They last a long time (about 5 weeks) and as they dry "turn" to resemble wood grain that can be stained or left natural. I've offered a video link so that you can watch me assemble the "*Aspidistra Rose*". You'll learn better visually than you would with a written description. **Watch the video at: uBloom.com/AspidistraRose**

Turning Florida Foliage into "Flowers" is magical. It reminds me to look for unexpected ways to enhance my flower arrangements!

IDEA Tint-it! Craft stores sell translucent color sprays that can enhance your dried "woven-roses." Clear varnish type sprays will also shine and protect these leaf flowers.

FOLIAGE
10 Aspidistra Leaves per Flower

AND...
Craft Covered Wire

HINT *Aspidistra* leaves take weeks to dry. For best results, position your "flower" in a cool, dry, place away from light and out of water for several weeks.

Fun with Weaving Palm Leaves

Foliage has been the "greens behind the scenes" in flower arranging for so many years. Today, however, we are realizing that foliage is just as incredible as flowers. It is coming forward and becoming a star itself. Central Florida is home to my foliage farming friends that produce an amazing variety of *Ferns* and "all things green!"

    I was fortunate to study flower arranging under Phil Rulloda. Phil is a simply amazing flower artist that taught me numerous practical ways to advance my creative flower design skills. One of the amazing techniques I learned using foliage was to "weave" a *Palm Leaf* into an impressionistic nautilus shell. Weaving the *Palms* or trimming them into interesting shapes provided several interesting elements for this foliage arrangement.

    I've realized it's much easier to visualize the process than read about it, thus I've included a link to a video on uBloom.com you can use as a tutorial reference. This arrangement is a study in green, featuring green flowers and foliage only. It's relaxing, refreshing and oh-so textural!

TIP Crisp it up! "Harden off" foliage cut from your yard or garden, by placing in water and then into the refrigerator for several hours before arranging. This will "crisp" up the foliage and make it last longer.

Watch the video at: uBloom.com/WeavePalmLeaves

FLOWERS
10 Bells of Ireland
2 Green Banksia Protea
1 Green Ornamental Kale (Brassica)

FOLIAGE
10 Aspidistra Leaves
2 Miniature Myrtle
10 Palm Leaves

AND...
Green Glass Dish
Flower Foam

HINT Trim the edges of palm leaves with shears to create dynamic angles and shapes to accent your flower arrangement.

Fun with
Protea and Texture

Flower arranging is all about selecting the right elements. Pairing the perfect ribbon or texture with the ideal flower creates excitement in a flower arrangement. Burlap, for example, has an organic, natural feel. Pairing it with lace creates a dynamic, elegant and comfortable contrast.

My friend Seth, at Reliant Ribbon, is a second-generation ribbon manufacturer. He creates ribbons that stir my imagination. Ribbon inspires me, sometimes as much as flowers or foliage. The burlap and lace ribbon (from Reliant Ribbon) pictured here is not only made from American-made fabrics, it's also stitched and created in the USA! It's a rugged, elegant and organic ribbon.

King and Queen Protea possess the same rugged, elegant and organic qualities. Pairing these elements for a wedding bouquet and reception decoration creates natural harmony. The texture of the flowers mirrors that of the ribbon, while the groupings of flowers echo the lace patterns.

Creatively arranging flowers, foliage and ribbon brings a sense of style and grace to any occasion. That's yet another fun aspect of arranging flowers!

 TIP Protea have very large stems… and the Gala® Bouquet Holder is designed to accommodate large stems and large quantities of stems. A large Wedding Bouquet, merits the benefits of the large Gala Bouquet Holder. (Full disclosure: when I developed the Gala, I insisted on a large version for these very reasons.)

BOUQUET FLOWERS & FOLIAGE

Queen Protea
8 Brunnia
8 Polar Star Roses
8 White Wax Flower
6 Chocolate Nigella

Queen Protea Foliage

ARRANGEMENT FLOWERS & FOLIAGE

King Protea
5 Pink Peonies
4 Pink Spray Aster
4 Pink Lisianthus
4 "Olesya" Spray Roses
3 Pink Grevillea

King Protea Foliage
Grevillea Foliage

AND…

Large Gala Bouquet Holder
Burlap and Lace Ribbon
Metal Container
Flower Foam
Double Faced Tape

Fun with Waterproof Ribbon

Imagine a waterproof ribbon that is created to look like variegated "*Aspidstra*" leaves. Amazing, right? Well that's what my friend Seth from Reliant Ribbon showed me. Seth constantly amazes me with Reliant's depth and variety of unusual and unique ribbons. Naturally, I couldn't wait to use it.

The great benefit of this ribbon is that it's waterproof, opening the doors to many great creative opportunities. Also, this ribbon can be placed underwater (in the bubble bowl). This is ideal because it doesn't create bacteria while submerged, yet provides a naturalistic accent. My flowers and foliage can go into the water and will last longer because the water stays fresh and clean.

I take flowers to friends all the time, so I want to ensure they arrive in their natural beauty while remaining hydrated during the journey. I use a product called Arrive Alive® that provides a water source for my flowers during transportation. While it's "genius" I like to cover this mechanic with something to keep it from distracting from the flowers. This waterproof ribbon is perfect for that task. Just add a few pieces of double faced tape and–voilà!–it looks as if I wrapped the stems in foliage!

Thanks to friends like Seth – the ribbon guy – my flower arrangements look better and last even longer… Bravo!

TIP **Conceal the Source.** Camouflaging the Arrive Alive water source is easy. Place a few pieces of double-faced tape around the plastic bag and cover with any type of ribbon.

FLOWERS
3 Pink Peonies
3 Stems Phalenopsis Orchids
8 "Precious Moments" Roses
4 Wax Foliage

FOLIAGE
4 Miniature Israeli Pittosporum

AND...
Footed Bubble Bowl
"Aspid" Waterproof Ribbon

HINT Water for bouquets. Providing a water supply (like Arrive Alive) for a hand bouquet is ideal. This allows the flowers to maintain hydration during transportation.

Fun with Succulents

Succulent plants are characterized by their ability to hold water with a swollen appearance. I became infatuated with *Succulents* long ago. John Ward, our grower at Greens Greenhouses, loved *Succulents*. His favorites were "*Living Stones*" so named because they resemble rocks rather than plants. The fact that these plants looked more like plastic was very intriguing to me.

Echeveria are the most common types of *Succulents* and are used frequently in flower arrangements. These durable "Cacti" come in a variety of colors, shapes, sizes. Some even sport the occasional brightly-colored bloom.

I keep a dish of *Succulents* on hand for flower arranging. I place a layer of river rocks into a shallow glass dish and then place the *Succulents* on top of the rocks. I add a layer of water to the tray that settles between the rocks. The *Succulents* will send down tiny fibrous roots but the rocks prevent them from sitting in water and rotting. I can keep them for months in a tray like this in bright direct sunlight!

This arrangement is created with a neutral or "nude" color palette using different types of flowers in various "skin tone" colors and textures. The *Succulent* is a perfect addition and creates an interesting focal point to the arrangement.

FLOWERS
1 Peach Anthurium
1 Pink Cybidium Orchid
1 Milva Rose
1 Peach Stock
3 Amnesia Roses
2 Pink Nerine Lilies
2 Peach Hypericum
3 Scabiosa Pods

FOLIAGE
1 Pink/Grey Echeveria (Succulent)
2 Dusty Miller

AND...
Ceramic Pot
Flower Foam

TIP *Succulents* require very little water but lots of light. Low light conditions will cause stretching. However, that can be interesting as well.

Because they rarely have a long stem, I typically drive a wood pick or bamboo stake into the stem from the bottom to assist in adding *Succulents* to a flower arrangement. The moisture of the *Succulent* and soaked flower foam will swell the stake causing it to hold firmly. This technique allows you to place *Succulents* in arrangements, wedding bouquets, and vase arrangements, just about anywhere!

Succulents are also the Chinese Symbol for Wealth and Prosperity. Placing *Succulent* plants throughout your home supports positive Feng Shui, and provides living plants that require very little care.

Succulents usually far outlast the flowers in an arrangement. The best news is that charming *Succulent* can return to its "tray of rocks" to await another creative adventure in flower arranging!

Watch the videos at:
uBloom.com/SucculentCare and
uBloom.com/WireSucculents

HINT Metallic touch! *Succulents* can be sprayed with "Modern Metal Paints" from Design Master to create fun metallic accents in an arrangement or bouquet.

FAVORITE FLOWERS
SUCCLENTS

Succulent leaves are considered a symbol of money or gold coins. They are also the Chinese symbol for Wealth & Prosperity, and believed to bring good fortune.

Scientific Name: *Echeveria* (also known as "Hen & Chicks")

"*Echeveria* are the perfect combination of foliage and flower; similar in form to a *Gerbera* or *Rose*. These colorful, long-lasting *Succulents* are a welcome addition to any flower arrangement!"
 - J Schwanke

Colors range from Grey, Green, Pink, and Mauve to Lavender and Burgundy, even Black. Most maintain a round form with concentric circles of multiple leaves.

A single leaf when planted will create another entirely new plant.

Succulents will flower on short stalks with brightly colored flowers. They were named after the 18th Century Mexican botanical artist Atanasio Echeverría y Godoy.

Fun with Succulents

FLOWER ARRANGING
VESSELS

I love to fill my favorite vases with pretty flowers. Each vase is attached to fond memories; a celebrated event, a travel adventure, or a gift from a loved one.

I believe you should use your special, treasured vases instead of just storing them in a cabinet. I love the idea of selecting a favorite vase from a shelf. You will be compelled to ponder "the memories within" as you dust it off, and then fill it with flowers to be enjoyed by all.

Color is a wonderful reason to choose a specific container for your arrangement. Perhaps a vessel has a unique color that will complement or contrast with the flowers that are selected for your arrangement. Many times the texture of a basket attracts me. Mirroring a texture in flowers or foliage can also enhance your flower arrangement. Coordinating or contrasting the colors of the flowers will help ensure that your arrangements have maximum impact.

 TIP Before creating an arrangement in a vase... fill it with water to test for leaks.

SMART VASES

My friends at Garcia Group Glass create "Smart Vases." I call them this because they are designed to hold a large amount of water and have a narrow neck that aids in the flower arranging process. The narrow neck holds stems together naturally fanning out the blossoms in the vase. The large reservoir of water ensures plenty of hydration for the flowers.

Whichever vessel you choose for your arrangement... whether it's memorable, colorful, textural or smart... be sure it will successfully hold water. This will provide support both physically and artistically to your flower arrangement!

TIP Protect the Surface. Glass vases that are filled with ice-cold water or have been in refrigeration can "sweat." It's always a good idea to protect fine furnishings or delicate surfaces by placing your vase on a trivet or coaster.

IDEA Less is More. An interesting vessel can be complemented artistically with a simple flower or two; even a single leaf or branch.

 HINT Containers (baskets for example) that do not hold water can be lined with recycled plastic containers, fruit jars or tin cans that will hold water and/or flower foam.

Fun with Flowers

Fun with Orchid Plants

Orchids are wonderful decorations for your home. They also make wonderful centerpieces for your dining table. I love them. However *Orchid* Plants used to intimidate me. I would get them and rapidly kill them. Depressing. Then I learned an amazing tip from my friend Toine while we were filming at Westerlay Orchids.

Placing a few ice cubes into your *Orchid* pot every few days will provide adequate moisture that will be absorbed by the plant as the ice melts. It's brilliant. It changed my life and extended the life of my *Orchids*! The *Orchids* thrived and I was thrilled.

Orchids come in a wide variety of colors, shapes and sizes. The *Orchids* shown in the photo are *"Butterfly"* Orchids (or *Phalenopsis*) named after their butterfly resemblance. (They also come in a miniature version).

Here, I've placed the pots in glass containers atop river rocks. It's a fun way to achieve a multi-level "tablescape" and coordinate the *Orchid* pots with my candles. The candles are set in sand and accented with river rocks in similar glass containers. Grouping these glass containers, along with a few river rocks and *Orchids*, create a blissful tropical centerpiece.

Meet me in the islands!

FLOWERS
3 Orchid Plants

AND...
Ceramic Pots
Glass Cylinders and Bowls
Candles
Sand
Black Stones

HINT Setting candles in sand-filled glass containers is a safe way to display and burn them. Melting wax will be easy to clean up and never damage a fine finished surface.

Fun with Pumpkins

Decorating in the Fall, especially for Halloween, is one of my favorite activities. Why? Because I love *Pumpkins*! When I was a little boy in the Flower Shop, we hollowed out *Pumpkins* and filled them with flowers to sell.

Pumpkins pop up in different shapes, sizes and colors from small to huge. Today heirloom *Pumpkins*, white *Pumpkins*, green ones, even "warty" *Pumpkins* can be found at local Farmers' Markets.

A hollowed out *Pumpkin* makes an ideal container for a flower arrangement (you can place a recycled sour cream container or mason jar inside). Sometimes I just drop my flower foam inside the cleaned *Pumpkin*. Then I simply add the flowers.

For an extra kick of color, I've enhanced these *Pumpkins* with micro-fine glitter in Halloween colors.

TIP Heavy Spray! I sprayed "Glue for Glitter" heavily around the top of the *Pumpkin*, letting it drip down the sides. Then I coated it with orange micro-fine glitter for an elegant effect.

You can mask off the stem and coat it with glue and micro-fine glitter as well. I also like to paint *Pumpkins* in festive colors such as purple, chartreuse green or black. Halloween is definitely all about the decorating... BOO!

Watch the video at: uBloom.com/Pumpkins

FLOWERS

5 Milva Roses
3 Purple Alstroemeria
3 Green Button Pompons
5 Orange Hypericum

AND...

Pumpkin
Glue for Glitter
Orange Micro-Fine Glitter

HINT Add the top to your arrangement by placing a bamboo stake into the *Pumpkin* top, and then simply add to your arrangement.

Fun with Pumpkins

Fun with Recycling Wine Bottles

I enjoy wine, so I accumulate a lot of wine bottles. I'm also an avid recycler and love opportunities to repurpose containers for my flower creations. Wine bottles are perfect single flowers vases. With a little creativity, it's simple to create a collection of flower vases for your next party.

Soak the wine bottles in soap and water to easily remove the labels. Then mask off the bottles in different patterns using quick-release painters tape. This takes the most amount of time, but doing it carefully will yield awesome results.

After the paint is dry to the touch, remove the tape. I love this part; your inner artist shines as you reveal the contrast of clear glass to the metallic paint.

Fill your "art vases" with flower food treated water, flowers and foliage. I added ColorFresh® painted foliage from FernTrust. ColorFresh lasts incredibly long, and the paint prevents shedding. You can also create your own by spraying different types of foliage from the yard or garden with Design Master® paint.

The collection of vases, mixed with flowers makes a fun centerpiece for a wine tasting, anniversary party or friendly get-together. **Watch the video at: uBloom.com/WIneBottles**

HINT Personalize your Bottle. Create your own touches using a permanent marker with a date, signature or event. This will transform your creations into one-of-their-kind keepsakes.

TIP Spray several light coats of paint; allowing each to dry, rather than one heavy coat. This covers the complete surface faster, while minimizing unsightly runs on the paint surface.

FLOWERS
3 Yellow Pincushion Protea
5 Craspedia (Globe Yarrow)
5 "Peach Avalanche" Roses

FOLIAGE
3 Salal Leaves
   (Etched with Silver Paint)
3 Ming Fern (Painted Silver)
3 Leatherleaf (Painted Gold)
10 Bear Grass (Painted Gold)

AND...
6 Empty Wine Bottles
   (labels removed)
Quick Release Tape
Metallic Spray Paint

Fun with Christmas Flowers

Flowers are a fun, festive way to make your Holidays – Merry and Bright!

As you walk amidst the twinkling lights this special season, humming "It's the Most Wonderful Time of the Year" nothing says Christmas like flowers! I also have "My Favorite Things" — quoting another famous Holiday Song — when it comes to arranging flowers for Christmas.

The perfect vase, matched with aromatic holiday foliage and flowers, is always a wonderful gift or centerpiece. The arrangement I featured here is created in my favorite vase, the "Rio Caché" from my friends at Garcia Group Glass. It's 100% post-consumer recycled glass and it's designed to hold flowers perfectly.

I filled the vase with *Sugar Pine*, *Cedar*, *Winterberry (Ilex)*, *Pine Cones*, *Variegated Holly*, and of course, *Red Carnations*. For me, nothing says Christmas more profoundly than *Red Carnations*. It's a family tradition!

I added a few red glass ornaments and finished the vase with one of my favorite ribbons from Reliant Ribbon. Seth — the ribbon guy — created this green burlap with a rugged organic feeling. It's the perfect accessory to wrap around the neck of the Rio Caché vase and the finishing touch for your Holiday celebration. **Watch the video at: uBloom.com/FavoriteThings**

HINT Zap the Sap! Pine sap can be sticky and difficult to remove from your hands or surfaces. Spray your sticky hands with Chrysal Leaf Shine, rub vigorously and simply wipe off with a paper towel.

FLOWERS
25 Red Carnations

FOLIAGE
5 Variegated Holly
5 Ilex Berry (aka Winterberry)
5 Port Orford Cedar
5 Sugar Pine

AND...
Rio Caché Vase
2 Yards Green Burlap Ribbon
5 Pine Cones
5 Red Glass Ornaments

Fun with Fragrant Flowers

It's important that flowers have fragrance, for the sake of memories. Flowers "should" smell like flowers. However, so many varieties these days have been hybridized for longer vase life. Many times, however, the fragrance is left behind with that process. *Roses* are an example of this loss. Many of the unique colors or unusually shaped *Roses* we see today have been 'bred' for color, to have fewer thorns, or to last much longer. Sadly, when we place these flowers to our nose, there is little or no fragrance!

I gravitate toward fragrant flowers because I love the smell of flowers. During a recent visit to Rose Story Farms in California, I learned a wonderful tip that allows you to enjoy the entire "fragrance experience." Deliberately smelling your flower allows you to experience the complex nature (notes) of the fragrance.

Smell for 5 seconds. Concentrate, close your eyes, and smell a flower (or any fragrance) for the 5 full seconds… the fragrance will be more likely to imprint on your memory for years to come.

This process is remarkable. The flowers on these pages have definitely imprinted themselves on my memory. They transport me to special celebrations and experiences in my life. The fragrance taps into my senses and brings joy. That's what flowers do for me.

FRAGRANT FLOWERS
Stemmed Gardenias
Lily of the Valley
"Sweet Moments" Roses
"Anuhea Spray" Roses
Stock
Freesia
Oriental Lilies
Carnations
Peonies
Lavendar

FRAGRANT FOLIAGE
Eucalyptus
Myrtle
Agonis
Lemon Cypress
Rosemary

HINT Fragrant flowers release more scent at room temperature. Flowers kept in coolers or refrigerators will hinder its natural fragrance.

The *Stemmed Gardenias* arranged in a vase (shown, page 130) are the brilliant idea of my childhood friend Robert Kitayama at KB Farms in Watsonville, California. Robert experienced the concept of *Stemmed Gardenias* on a trip to Hawaii. Locals would cut the stems with blossoms and buds intact from bushes and then place them in a vase. Much to his surprise each and every blossom opened... with fragrant perfection!

The *Lily of the Valley* (shown, page 131) was cut from my backyard. I love those magical days in May when my precious plants burst into blooms with tiny scented bell shaped blossoms. Nothing compares to the smell of fresh *Lily of Valley*... these flowers are intoxicating!

I also included *"Sweet Moments" Roses* from Eufloria Flowers that possess the Rose fragrance we all treasure. For me it's the perfumed blossoms of my Grandmother's *Rose* bush or the smell of *Roses* blooming in our *Rose* Greenhouses when I was a kid. While not as long-lasting as recent hybrids; *"Sweet Moments" Roses* make up for it with their ability to scent an entire room!

The *Stock* blossoms provide a clove-based flower fragrance. That fragrance still brings me back to the fields of blooming *Stock* in Lompoc, California. It's the sweet smell paired with the beauty of flowers that touches my soul.

Remember, fragrance is not limited to flowers, fragrant foliage exists as well. My favorites include *Eucalyptus* and *Myrtle* that grow in patchwork-like fields at Mellano's in Oceanside, California. The Mellano family has perfected foliage production over generations. My friend Michelle tells the story of how her father's hands would smell like *Eucalyptus* after a day of harvesting. Today that fragrance is a constant reminder of her amazing flower-farming father.

Believe in the power of a fragrant flower. Their ability to stir our memories or create new ones is simply profound.

FAVORITE FLOWERS
STEMMED GARDENIA

"I'm often asked what my favorite flower is... a *Stemmed Gardenia* represents many of the attributes I love about Flowers, including their famous fragrance. Grown by my childhood friend Robert Kitayama, these *Gardenias* are close to perfection... residing in a vase!"
— J Schwanke

Named after Dr. Alexander Garden (1730-1791) A Scottish born American Naturalist.

A genus of 142 species of flowering plants in the *Coffee* Family!

The *Gardenia* is heavily scented, this sweet fragrance is memorable, classic and timeless. Everyone knows the scent of *Gardenias*.

Stemmed Gardenias are grown in the USA by KB Farms in Watsonville, CA.

Stemmed Gardenias will last for 5-7 days in a vase. Blossoms and buds will open fully, the blossom is originally white but changes to warm ivory tone as the bud fades.

Fun with Stemmed Gardenia

Fun with Art and Flowers

Each flower is a wonderful work of art... waiting silently in colorful beauty... for us to enjoy.

I cannot deny that arranging flowers is fun. As you gain more confidence and explore your natural talents and creativity, it's likely you'll begin to create arrangements that many will consider "Flower Art".

Fine Art Museums across the country hold "flower events," such as "Bouquets to Art" in San Francisco or "Art in Bloom" at the Boston Museum of Fine Art. These unique annual events paved the way for dozens of others where "Flower Artistry" is combined with permanent displays of "Fine Art." Many times local flower designers interpret permanent pieces of art through flower design at these Museum gatherings... it's breathtaking.

I've shared my "Fun with Flowers" presentations at many of these events. It is so enjoyable to share my love of flowers, fun stories and creativity with the audiences. This arrangement is from an "Art in Bloom" event in my hometown of Grand Rapids, Michigan.

Implementing the elements and principles of design into my flower arrangements allows me to create fun-filled flower works of art. Much like a painting or sculpture, the flowers allow me (and you) to combine textures, line, focal area, color and space into a... living artistic arrangement.

 HINT Never cut Freesia! Freesia has the strongest vascular system of any flower so when you purchase a bunch of freesia, do not re-cut. Simply unbundle and place into cold water with flower food. This will ensure that every blossom will open fully.

FLOWERS
10 Orange Freesia
10 Yellow Stock
10 Yellow Parrot Tulips
5 Peach Parrot Tulips
3 Stems of Jazzabelle Spray Roses
10 Leucadendron
3 Yellow Spray Chrysanthemum

FOLIAGE
5 Flax Leaves
5 Podocarpus
5 "Star" Asparagus Sprengeri
5 Red Huckleberry

AND...
Various Fruit
Resin Urn
3 Block of Flower Foam

FLOWER RESOURCES

DECO BEADS BY JRM

These water storing gel accents create glimmering flower or candle arrangements in clear vases and bowls. Three styles for all decorating tastes: Crystal Accents and Deco Beads for traditional and Deco Cubes for contemporary. Ideal for candle, silk and fresh flower arrangements. Perfect for weddings, birthdays, parties, graduations and much more.

Easy to use - just add water. Layer your favorite colors for stunning effects

Available in clear and a rainbow of 12 standard colors. Non-toxic and environmentally safe. Deco Beads, Cubes and Accents swell up to more than 1/2 inch. Introducing 20 new exciting colors.

soilmoist.com/products/decobeads.php

DESIGN MASTER

Design Master offers color sprays and accessory products for the many unique applications demanded by creative professionals and imaginative individuals for floral and decorative projects. The unique features of our sprays let you control the nuance of color. Whether using color straight-from-the-can, layering it in light veils or incorporating it in one of our simple finish techniques... you design the spirit of color. dmcolor.com

CHRYSAL AMERICAS

Chrysal takes pride in creating excellence in care for cut flowers. We care for flowers, from harvest until the moment they bloom in a vase. For each phase in the life of a cut flower, Chrysal offers just the right product for long lasting beauty.

www.chrysalusa.com

FLOWER RESOURCES

FERNTRUST

FernTrust, Inc. of Seville, Florida is a cooperative of quality oriented growers sharing a rich history in agri-business. Acting as a cooperative allows the grower-members to focus on growing the highest quality foliage available. Together these growers have decades of experience. FernTrust offers over 300 unique products including famous FernCool leatherleaf along with the spectacular ColorFresh Foliage line and the versatile Fabulous Foliage Bouquets. **ferntrust.com**

RESENDIZ BROTHERS PROTEA GROWERS

Resendiz Brothers grows, harvests and ships over 200 varieties of South African and Australian flowers and plants. Known for their exceptional value and long vase life, our products create a dramatic impact when placed in arrangements, bouquets or displays. We guarantee the freshness and quality of everything we ship. We are confident you will be pleased. **resendizbrothers.com**

ARRIVE ALIVE

Arrive Alive, a patent pending floral hydration system, extends the life and beauty of cut flower arrangements and bouquets. Arrive Alive provides a constant water source to delicate cut flowers during transit or shipment. It is easy to use and cost-effective, increasing customer satisfaction and repeat business.
arrivealiveproducts.com

EUFLORIA FLOWERS

Eufloria Flowers has been a premier grower of varietal roses for over seven generations. Our flowers are of rare quality and performance, and are consistently recognized as the most beautiful roses throughout the industry. We have pioneered and perfected hydroponic growing methods that enable Eufloria Flowers to set a standard for quality and innovation. **eufloriaflowers.com**

FLOWER RESOURCES

ROSEVILLE FARMS

Clematis vines produce excellent cut flowers, which last 10 days or more in a vase. Roseville Farms is the only Clematis nursery in the world to offer large flowering vine-type Clematis as cut flowers. Clematis stems are very sturdy, and therefore pack and ship very well to locations all over North America and Europe. Roseville Farms utilizes its yearly production rotation of millions of Clematis plants to produce large numbers of cut stems weekly for up to eight months of the year. We offer five color Categories: White, Red, Blue, Purple, and Pink.

We currently grow more than 80 varieties of Clematis, and are constantly testing these varieties to make certain that we are offering only the best, longest-lasting varieties in our cut flower production.

rosevillefarms.com

ALPHA FERN

Established in 1975, and a founding member of the Florida Leatherleaf Growers Association; Alpha Fern Company continues to grow and expand their incredibly diverse foliage offerings including unique wreath, garland, and centerpiece designs created by their exclusive design team. Alpha Fern's signature world class foliage is American Grown and shipped throughout North America and the World.

alphafern.net

GARCIA GROUP GLASS

The finest glassware vases for flower arranging come from Garcia Group Glass. American-made FloraGlas and 100% post-consumer Recycled G3 Glass highlight these creative and well-designed vases. Garcia Group Glass continues to create innovative, unique and quality glass products for professional florists and flower arranging enthusiasts throughout North America. Find Garcia Group Glass:

www.ubloom.com/GarciaGlass

FLOWER RESOURCES

SUN VALLEY GROUP

The Sun Valley commitment is simple, to create the best floral experience through operational excellence. Combining a commitment to quality control, state-of-the-art technologies, the best bulb and flower stock, superb growing conditions, and a workforce of dedicated team members, Sun Valley brings flowers to market, Creating a World of Color. thesunvalleygroup.com

OCEAN VIEW FLOWERS

We have a passion for quality. Ocean View Flowers is located in the Lompoc Valley, near the Pacific Ocean. The valley's unique physical characteristics make it one of the finest flower growing regions in California. Cool ocean breezes help provide excellent growing and harvesting conditions for all our varieties. Our practices and our people combine to produce the highest quality fresh cut flowers. oceanviewflowers.com

MELLANO & COMPANY

Since 1925, Mellano & Company has established an enduring tradition of innovation. Our farms include more than 375 acres in San Luis Rey and Carlsbad, California, including the famous Carlsbad flower fields. Produced under the care of two PhDs and a Master-level Horticulturalist, our crops are grown under the most advanced scientific and environmentally responsible conditions. mellano.com

ACOLYTE

Acolyte Technologies Corp. designs and manufactures battery operated LED lighting products specifically for the floral and event industry, including but not limited to weddings, parties and special events. Let Acolyte products bring a beautiful and original glow to your next event!

888acolyte.com

FLOWER RESOURCES

ESPRIT MIAMI

Esprit Miami is a leading provider of fresh cut flowers. Esprit has developed a long-standing reputation for high quality, innovative products and outstanding customer service. Esprit keeps a watchful eye on trends in cut flowers by visiting breeders and growers around the world every year. Our flowers mean business.

espritmiami.com

RELIANT RIBBON

With over 17,000 in stock items, Reliant Ribbon provides a nearly endless selection of trend-wise and fashion forward ribbons that can be delivered fast. With 3 convenient ways to order (Sales Reps, Customer Service or Website) Reliant Ribbon offers the very best in service and selection.

reliantribbon.com

KB FARMS

Kitayama Brothers has been growing and shipping beautiful cut flowers from Northern California since 1948. Located on majestic Monterey Bay, the KB Farms' Watsonville location is known for its perfect flower growing conditions for the approximately 20 different flowers and cut greens produced. Our product selection makes us a top choice for wedding and event professionals from around the country. kbflowers.com

BRANNAN STREET WHOLESALE FLORIST

Not only are SF Brannan Street flowers a feast for the eyes… they provide consistent quality and constant variety. Specializing in novelty items such as flowering, fruiting branches, vines, garden and imported roses, domestic field flowers as well as exotic blooms and foliages from around the world. SF Brannan Street ships to retail and wholesale florists nationwide.

brannanst.com

FLOWER RESOURCES

ACCENT DECÓR

Founded with a passion for inspiring through design, and committed to quality and innovation, each season we scour the globe to build new collections on the leading edge of today's trends, to deliver our customers the best new products. This commitment to excellence has built a company that holds the industry standard for providing beautiful floral-ware, containers, glassware, ceramics, accessories and exceptional customer service. **accentdecor.com**

WM F. PUCKETT INC.

Wm F. Puckett is a 3rd Generation professional grower and distributor of floral greens. A Pioneer in the Hydroseal process (which seals in moisture and extends shelf life), Wm F. Puckett is the only grower to use Hydroseal as prescribed by cut foliage post harvest scientists, thus setting the standard of excellence for cut foliage. Ask about Puckett's custom garlands, wreaths, swags and other quality foliage.

puckettfern.com

UBLOOM RESOURCE GUIDE

Find Flowers, Foliage and Flower Arranging Supplies near you...

All of the wonderful flowers, foliage, tools, containers and accessories featured in J's *Fun with Flowers* projects throughout this book are available through local resources, flower sellers and distributors all across the USA.

Find your nearest local resource – visit uBloom's free Professional Resource Directory at **www.uBloom.com/ResourceGuide**

Choose the product you're looking for and select your State from the results provided. You'll be able to locate your local resource for flowers, foliage, supplies and much more! Each Resource listing provides the Company Name, Address, Phone, Fax and Web-address. uBloom.com makes it easy to find local resources for flowers, foliage and flower arranging supplies.

ACKNOWLEDGEMENTS

I've never considered "Flowers" work... Flowers have always been "Fun." Luckily all of the jobs I've had throughout my life have included flowers, thus "work" always was and continues to be "Fun!"

    Surrounding yourself with people that can help you "Get your 'Fun' done" is crucial. This book was a whole lot of fun for me... yet it took a great deal of "work" by truly talented people to get it done! I am extremely thankful for these Professional Individuals that happen to also be among my friends and flower family:

Pam McCormick (who actually directed my very first video "Unlocking the Secrets of Wedding Design") edited "Fun with Flowers." Pam helped me tame a great deal of "writing demons" yet magically kept my personality intact. Everyone always thanks the editor for making him or her sound smarter, more professional and wise... because it's VERY, VERY TRUE!

Debra Prinzing, my book mentor, who couldn't figure out WHY I didn't have a Flower book. Debra "held my hand" and encouraged me through the process. She listened, advised and ultimately helped me make this "dream come true."

Dan Norman, the expert when it comes to printing. This book is a testament to his attention to detail, expertise and friendship!

Dean van Dis, **Andrew Maguire** and **Joe Matteson**, the photographers who allowed you to see the beautiful flowers in all their glory are amazing. They are Talented and Professional Flower Photographers, who are always willing to take "just one more shot."

Chris, Keith, Brad, Deano, and the JTV/uBloom Crew, always get the shot, make the cut and deliver magic. If you loved the video links and website, you'll join in me in thanking this incredible, patient, and talented crew.

My Flower Farmer Friends, who grew the pretty flowers seen in this book. If folks only knew how many hours of sweat, sunshine and passion are required to grow a beautiful flower, they would gladly pay the price.

My Flower Industry Friends that make the ribbon, vases, flower food, tools, and other amazing accessories that help me create "Flowers Fantastic!" They are constantly creating, inventing the next "new" thing...

My Mother, and her wonderful photographic archive and memory; plus the **Greens** and **Schwankes**... who have been "turning people's feelings into flowers" for generations.

Kelly... there's not enough room to THANK YOU for all the hours, details, checks, switches, fixes, special touches and love you add to this and every project I dream up. You are the "Oracle"...

CONTRIBUTORS

KELLY BLANK
Art Direction and Design

Graphic Design, Illustration, uBloom video producer and an occasional flower arrangement describes the majority of assignments for Kelly at Blank Art and Design. Kelly has been designing and art directing for 20+ years for clients within and outside of the flower industry. He enjoys a balance of Travel and Homelife with J and their 2 dogs.

kelly@blankartanddesign.com

DEAN VAN DIS
Photographer

Dean Van Dis is a commercial and editorial photographer whose old school value of hard work has seen him through even the most challenging photo shoots. His work has taken him around the world and has appeared in several national and international design magazines. He lives in Grand Rapids, Michigan. See his work at deanvandis.com.

ANDREW MAGUIRE
Photographer

Andrew can usually be found bouncing between the Rocky Mountains of Colorado and beautiful West Michigan shooting for a range of clients from Nike Footwear, Ford Motor to JTV/uBloom! The adventures and opportunities to explore new places and cultures are the driving forces behind Andrew's work. Check out his latest adventures at andrew-maguire.com

JOE MATTESON
Photographer

Born and raised in White Lake, Michigan. Joe earned his Associates in Photography from Lansing Community College. Joe moved to Grand Rapids and was connected with Dean Van Dis who ultimately introduced Joe to the great people at JTV/uBloom. Joe currently resides in Austin, Texas shooting portraits, architecture and events.

joematteson.com

Fun with Flowers – Contributors

MORE ABOUT UBLOOM.COM

I love sharing... especially when it comes to flowers, so I created **uBloom.com**. All across America and in over 100 countries people visit uBloom.com to learn more about Flower Arranging online!

Some of the resources available at uBloom.com:

- Over 500 "How to Arrange Flowers" videos for any occasion
- "Flowers 101" – education & information for beginners
- uBloom Flower Guide w/100's of Flowers and their meanings
- Over 1,000 Fresh Cut Videos: tips, tricks, & arrangement ideas
- Clips from my TV appearances/stage presentations
- Documentaries about America's Flower and Foliage Farmers
- Blogs, including "The Flower Stand" by yours truly
- NEW "Fun with Flowers & J" Show posted weekly

uBloom.com is for anyone that loves Flowers!

Much of the information is free. You can download "how to videos" similar to those in this book for a dollar or two. Or – become an "All-inclusive uBloom Club Member for only $30 a year. Even if you don't join, uBloom is a creative resource and a fun place to visit. **We're having Fun with Flowers every day!**

Sign up for J's Flower Thoughts. www.ubloom.com/flowerthoughts
Daily Emails Monday-Friday sharing tips, tricks and fun with flowers.

Visit J's Website www.uBloom.com
Visit J's Blog www.ubloom.com/blogs/j
J's Live Appearances www.ubloom.com/j/schedule
Twitter www.twitter.com/jschwanke
Facebook www.facebook.com/jschwankeflowers
Pinterest www.pinterest.com/jschwanke
Instagram www.instagram.com/ubloom

144 Fun with Flowers – uBloom.com